Love Match

Comparing Times and Cultures

Edited by

Cecily O'Neill

Published by Collins Educational, an imprint of HarperCollins*Publishers* Ltd,
77–85 Fulham Palace Road, London W6 8JB

www.**Collins**Education.com
On-line support for schools and colleges

© Selection and Activities copyright Cecily O'Neill 2002

First published 2002

ISBN 000 713558 0

British Library Cataloguing in Publication Data

A catalogue record for this book is available from the British Library.

Commissioned by Isabelle Zahar, edited by Mark Dudgeon, picture research by
Sarah McNaught and Mark Dudgeon

Design by Jordan Publishing Design, cover design by Jordan Publishing Design,
cover photograph of *The Taming of the Shrew* courtesy of The Ronald Grant Archive.

Acknowledgements
The following permissions to reproduce material are gratefully acknowledged:
Photographs: The Ronald Grant Archive, p.15; Zoë Dominic, p.43; Zoë Dominic, p.66;
Theatre Royal Stratford East Archives, p.82.
Text Extracts: Hobson's Choice by Harold Brighouse courtesy of Samuel French Ltd on
behalf of the Estate of Harold Brighouse; *Brecht Collected Plays: Seven*, ed. John Willett
and Ralph Manheim, Methuen Publishing Ltd; *A Taste of Honey*, Methuen Publishing
Ltd; *Joan's Book*, by Joan Littlewood, Methuen Publishing Ltd, p.88–89;
AQA Specifications are reproduced by permission of the Assessment and
Qualifications Alliance, p.2, 3.

Every effort has been made to trace copyright holders, but in some cases this has
proved impossible. The publishers would be happy to hear from any copyright
holder that has not been acknowledged.

Production by Katie Morris, printed and bound in Thailand by Imago
Public performance of the *Hobson's Choice* extract must be licensed by Samuel
French Ltd, 52 Fitzroy Street, London W1T 5JR.

Contents

KEY	
◁ 71–74 71–74 ▷	cross-reference between playscript and teaching resources.
(H)	in resources = activity suitable for homework.

Introduction

This book contains 4 extracts from classic plays of different periods, one written before 1914 and three from the 20th century. The text covers the requirements of the new GCSE Drama Specifications, providing an ideal resource for coursework. The scenes are all concerned with courtship and marriage and the accompanying activities explore these and related topics in depth. These activities involve the study of different times and cultures, encourage connections and comparisons between texts, and promote an awareness of the context and background of the plays. In addition, they offer students opportunities to:

1 "demonstrate knowledge and understanding of the use of dramatic techniques to explore ideas and issues and of different ways of conveying action, character, atmosphere and tension" (AQA);

2 "demonstrate ability in and knowledge and understanding of the practical skills in drama necessary for the realization of a presentation to an audience" (AQA);

3 "analyse and evaluate the effectiveness of their own and others' work" (AQA & Edexcel).

Ideas for improvisation, performance, written work and discussion are supplemented by a section on comparative work and on technical and design ideas, and cover the range of assessment options for coursework and exploratory study. An outline of the skills covered by each extract can be found at the end of this introduction. Opportunities to fulfill many of the learning requirements of the English Framework have also been highlighted in the resource material with the key aims referenced to the English Framework.

Whether used for GCSE Drama study or Key Stage 3 work in Drama or English, *Love Match* provides a stimulating and enriching resource for the study of classic drama.

AQA DRAMA COURSEWORK COVERAGE CHART

Candidates of the AQA Drama GCSE course must offer two different options for coursework, one from the list of Scripted Work options and one from the list of Unscripted Work options. At least one of these must be a performance option. Where a technical and design skill option is undertaken it must contribute to a group performance. Each option is divided into three parts, with each part testing a different Assessment Objective (AO):

1 **Response to plays and other types of drama**, in which candidates' ability to *"respond with knowledge and understanding to plays and other types of drama from a performance perspective and to explore relationships and comparisons between texts and dramatic styles of different periods and of different cultures in order to show an awareness of their social context and genre"* is assessed (AO2);

2 **Work in progress**, in which candidates' ability to *"analyse and evaluate the effectiveness of their own and others' work with sensitivity as they develop and present their work in an appropriate format for communication"* is assessed (AO3);

3 **Final presentation (either performance or demonstration/artefact(s))**, in which candidates' ability to *"demonstrate ability in and knowledge and understanding of the practical skills in drama necessary for the realisation of a presentation to an audience, working constructively with others"* is assessed (AO1) (AQA).

AQA c/w option	1. The Taming of the Shrew	2. Hobson's Choice	3. The Caucasian Chalk Circle	4. A Taste of Honey	Comparing the Four Extracts & GCSE Drama sections
Option 1: Devised thematic work	B, C, D, F, G, H, I	C, E, F, H, K, N	C, D, E	B, D, E, F, G, H	A, B, C, D, E, F, G, H, I, J, K, L, p.102
Option 2: Acting	A, D, H		B, C, E		A, p.102
Option 3: Improvisation	B, G	C, E, H, K, N		B, D, E, F, G, H	A, B, C, D, F, J
Option 6: Set	p.14	p.42	p.64	p.82	p.104
Option 7: Costume	p.14	p.43	p.65	p.83	p.104
Option 8: Make-up					p.106
Option 9: Properties				p.83	p.108
Option 10: Masks			p.65		p.106
Option 11: Puppets					p.107
Option 12: Lighting		p.43			p.109
Option 13: Sound	p.14	p.43	p.65	p.83	p.110
Option 14: Stage management	*	*	*	*	p.108

* All of these texts are suitable for the Stage Management option

EDEXCEL DRAMA COURSEWORK COVERAGE CHART

The chart below highlights which activities and pages provide opportunities or guidance for work on the different components of Edexcel Paper 1 Unit 1: Drama Exploration. In the workshop for this paper, to be based around at least 2 different types of drama texts, candidates are required to use at least 4 of the explorative strategies (a), at least 2 of the skill areas (b), and to select and use appropriately the elements of drama (c) in their responses to the stimulus material.

Edexcel c/w strategies, skills and elements of drama	1. The Taming of the Shrew	2. Hobson's Choice	3. The Caucasian Chalk Circle	4. A Taste of Honey	Comparing the Four Extracts & GCSE Drama sections
(a) Explorative Strategies					
Still image			E	B	C, K
Thought-tracking		F		B	
Narrating			D	H	E, L
Hot-seating	C				
Role-play	B	C, E, H, N	B	D, E, H	D, F, L
Cross-cutting					J
Forum-theatre		K		E	
Marking the moment			E	B	
(b) The Drama Medium					
Use of costume, masks, make-up	p.14	p.43	p.65	p.83	p.104, 106
Sound/music	p.14	p.43	p.65	p.83	L, p.110
Lighting		p.43	E		L, p.109
Space/levels			D		
Set and props	D, p.14	p.42	p.64	p.82, 83	p.104, 108
Movement, mime, gesture	B, D	D, E, F	B	B, D, E, H	L
Voice			B, D	G	L
Spoken language	B, C, D	D, E, F	B, D	B, D, E, G, H	L
(c) The Elements of Drama					
Action/plot/content	A, C, H	A, B, D, G, J	A	A, B, C	B, M
Forms	C, F, G	A	A, D		E, M
Climax/anticlimax	C				E
Rhythm/pace/tempo			D		E
Contrasts		L, M	D	A	B
Characterisation		A, B, D, J	B	B, G	
Conventions	C, D	L	D	G	M
Symbols				H	M

The Taming of the Shrew

William Shakespeare

WILLIAM SHAKESPEARE

William Shakespeare was born in Stratford upon Avon in 1564, the eldest son of John Shakespeare, a prosperous grain and leather merchant. He probably attended the local grammar school where Greek and Latin would have been the basis of his education.

At the age of 18, he married Anne Hathaway, and by 1585 they had three children, two daughters, and a son, Hamnet, who died in childhood. By 1591 Shakespeare had moved to London and was working as an actor and a playwright. We do not know what prompted his move to London or his choice of career. By 1593 he was acting and writing for two London companies. By 1594 he was a leading member of a new company, The Lord Chamberlain's Men. This was a permanent group of players, probably composed of 12 to 15 adult actors and several boys who played the female roles.

By the early 1600's, Shakespeare was among the foremost of English playwrights. He had written popular pastoral comedies – *A Midsummer Night's Dream* and *As you Like It*, as well as history plays such as *Henry V* and *Richard III*. Later he produced his greatest tragedies – *Hamlet*, *Othello*, *Macbeth* and *King Lear*. Shakespeare retired from the stage around 1607 and returned to New Place, Stratford. He had made enough money to become a landowner and acquire a coat-of-arms, which recognised that he was now a 'gentleman'. He continued to write, producing a number of tragi-comedies, including *The Winter's Tale* and *The Tempest*. He wrote nothing during the last four years of his life and died in 1616, aged 52.

SUMMARY OF THE PLOT

A wealthy gentleman of Padua, Baptista Minola, has two daughters, Bianca and Katherine. Bianca, who is sweet-natured, has a number of suitors, but her father refuses to allow her to marry until her sister Katherine has found a husband. Kate, the Shrew of the title, is so wilful and aggressive that nobody wants to marry her. Petruchio, a poor country gentleman, has come to Padua in search of a rich wife. His friend Hortensio, who is in love with Bianca, tells him about Kate, but warns him about her personality. Petruchio, who is only interested in money, gets Baptista's permission to woo her. His plan is to ignore her behaviour and respond as if she finds his proposal acceptable.

After winning Baptista's permission to marry his daughter Petruchio plans to tame Kate by humiliating her and behaving even more wilfully than she does. First he arrives late for the wedding dressed in ridiculous clothes. Then he whisks her off to his dilapidated country house. He finds fault with everything and claims that nothing in the house is good enough for her. He deprives her of food and sleep while apparently wanting only the best of everything for her, and eventually, worn out and hungry, Kate eventually gives in and submits to him.

When they return to Padua, Bianca is married to Lucentio and Hortensio has married a rich widow. The three bridegrooms make a bet to discover which of their wives is most obedient. To everyone's surprise, Kate proves the most submissive and Petruchio wins the bet.

THE SCENE IN CONTEXT

In this scene, Petruchio meets Kate for the first time. She treats him with contempt, and even violence, but in spite of this he pretends that he finds her courteous and gentle, and overrides all her objections. Baptista accepts Petruchio's word that Kate has agreed to marry him, although she continues to object violently to the marriage.

The Taming of the Shrew

By

William Shakespeare

CAST LIST

BAPTISTA a gentleman of Padua
KATHERINE one of his daughters
PETRUCHIO a gentleman of Venice, a suitor to Katherine
GREMIO a suitor to Bianca, Baptista's younger daughter
TRANIO a servant to Lucentio, who is love with Bianca

ACT TWO
Scene One

*The house of **Baptista**, a merchant of Padua.*

BAPTISTA Signior Petrucio, will you go with us,
Or shall I send my daughter Kate to you?

PETRUCHIO I pray you do. (*exeunt all but **Petrucio***)
I'll attend her here,
And woo her with some spirit when she comes.
Say that she rail; why then I'll tell her plain
She sings as sweetly as a nightingale.
Say that she frown; I'll say she looks as clear
As morning roses newly wash'd with dew.
Say she'll be mute, and will not speak a word;
Then I'll commend her volubility,
And say she uttereth piercing eloquence.
If she do bid me pack, I'll give her thanks,

As though she bid me stay by her a week;
If she deny to wed, I'll crave the day.
When I shall as the bans, and when be married.
But here she comes; and now Petrucio, speak.

(enter **Katherine***)*

Good morrow, Kate – for that's your name, I hear.

KATHERINE Well have you heard, but something hard of hearing:
They call me Katherine that do talk of me.

PETRUCHIO You lie, in faith, for you are called plain Kate,
And bonny Kate, and sometimes Kate the curst;
But, Kate, the prettiest Kate in Christendom,
Kate of Kate Hall, my super-dainty Kate,
For dainties are all Kates, and therefore, Kate,
Take this of me, Kate of my consolation –
Hearing thy mildness prais'd in every town,
Thy virtues spoke of, and they beauty sounded,
Yet not so deeply as to thee belongs,
Myself am mov'd to woo thee for my wife.

KATHERINE Mov'd! In good time! Let him that mov'd thee hither
Remove thee hence. I knew you at the first
You were a moveable.

PETRUCHIO Why, what's a moveable?

KATHERINE A joint-stool.

PETRUCHIO Thou hast hit it. Come, sit on me.

KATHERINE Asses are made to bear, and so are you.

PETRUCHIO Women are made to bear and so are you.

KATHERINE No such jade as you, if me you mean.

PETRUCHIO Alas, good Kate, I will not burden thee!
For knowing thee to be but young and light –

KATHERINE Too light for such a swain as you to catch;
And yet as heavy as my weight should be.

PETRUCHIO Should be! Should – buzz!

KATHERINE Well ta'en, and like a buzzard.

PETRUCHIO O slow-wing'd turtle, shall a buzzard take you?

KATHERINE Ay, for a turtle, as he takes a buzzard.

PETRUCHIO Come, come, you wasp; i'faith, you are too angry.

KATHERINE If I be waspish, best beware my sting.

PETRUCHIO My remedy is then to pluck it out.

KATHERINE Ay, if the fool could find it out.

PETRUCHIO Who knows not where a wasp does wear his sting?
    In his tail.

KATHERINE In his tongue.

PETRUCHIO Whose tongue?

KATHERINE Yours if you talk of tales; and so farewell.

PETRUCHIO What, with my tongue in your tail? Nay, come again.
    Good Kate, I am a gentleman.

KATHERINE That I'll try. (*she strikes him*)

PETRUCHIO I swear I'll cuff you, if you strike again.

KATHERINE So you may lose your arms.
    If you strike me, you are no gentleman;
    And if no gentleman, why then no arms.

PETRUCHIO A herald, Kate? O put me in thy books.

KATHERINE What is your crest – a cox-comb?

PETRUCHIO A combless cock, so Kate will be my hen.

KATHERINE No cock of mine; you crow too like a craven.

PETRUCHIO Nay. Come, Kate, come; you must not look so sour.

KATHERINE It is my fashion when I see a crab.

PETRUCHIO Why, here's no crab; and therefore look not sour.

KATHERINE There is, there is.

PETRUCHIO Then show it me.

KATHERINE Had I a glass I would.

PETRUCHIO What, you mean my face?

KATHERINE Well aim'd of such a young one.

PETRUCHIO Now, by Saint George, I am too young for you.

KATHERINE Yet you are wither'd.

PETRUCHIO 'Tis with cares.

KATHERINE I care not.

PETRUCHIO Nay, hear you, Kate – in sooth, you 'scape not so.

KATHERINE I chafe you, if I tarry; let me go.

PETRUCHIO No, not a whit; I find you passing gentle.
'Twas told to me you were rough, and coy, and sullen,
And now I find report a very liar;
For thou art pleasant, gamesome, passing courteous,
But slow in speech, yet sweet as spring-time flowers.
Thou canst not frown, thou canst not look askance,
Nor bite the lip, as angry wenches will,
Nor hast thou pleasure to be cross in talk;
But thou with mildness entertain'st thy wooers;
With gentle conference, soft and affable.
Why does the world report that Kate doth limp?
O sland'rous world! Kate like the hazel-twig
Is straight and slender, and as brown in hue
As hazel-nuts, and sweeter than the kernels.
O, let me see thee walk. Thou dost not halt.

KATHERINE Go, fool, and whom thou keep'st command.

PETRUCHIO Did ever Dian so become a grove
As Kate this chamber with her princely gait?
O, be thou Dian, and let her be Kate;
And then let Kate be chaste, and Dian sportful!

KATHERINE Where did you study all this goodly speech?

PETRUCHIO It is extempore, from my mother wit.

KATHERINE A witty mother! Witless else her son.

PETRUCHIO Am I not wise?

KATHERINE Yes, keep you warm.

PETRUCHIO Marry, so I mean, sweet Katherine, in thy bed.
And therefore, setting all this chat aside,
Thus in plain terms: your father hath consented
That you shall be my wife: your dowry 'greed on;
And will you, nill you, I will marry you.
Now, Kate, I am a husband for your turn;
For, by this light, whereby I see thy beauty,
Thy beauty that doth make me like thee well,
Thou must be married to no man but me;
For I am born to tame you, Kate,
And bring you from a wild Kate to a Kate
Conformable as other household Kates.

*(re-enter **Baptista**, **Gremio** and **Tranio**)*

Here comes your father. Never make denial;
I must and will have Katherine to my wife.

BAPTISTA Now, Signior Petruchio, how speed you with my
daughter?

PETRUCHIO How but well, sir? How but well?
It were impossible I should speed amiss.

BAPTISTA Why, how now, daughter Katherine, in your dumps?

KATHERINE Call you me daughter? Now I promise you
You have show'd a tender fatherly regard
To wish me wed to one half lunatic,
A mad-cap ruffian and a swearing Jack,
That thinks with oaths to face the matter out.

PETRUCHIO Father, 'tis thus: yourself and all the world
That talk'd of her have talk'd amiss of her.

If she be curst, it is for policy,
For she's not froward, but modest as the dove;
She is not hot, but temperate as the morn;
For patience she will prove a second Grissel,
And Roman Lucrece for her chastity.
And to conclude, we have 'greed so well together
That upon Sunday is the wedding-day.

KATHERINE I'll see thee hang'd on Sunday first.

GREMIO Hark, Petruchio; she says she'll see thee hanged first.

TRANIO Is this your speeding? Nay, then, good-night our part!

PETRUCHIO Be patient, gentlemen. I choose her for myself;
If she and I be pleas'd, what's that to you?
'Tis bargain'd 'twixt us twain, being alone,
That she shall still be curst in company.
I tell you 'tis incredible to believe
How much she loves me – O, the kindest Kate!
She hung about my neck, and kiss on kiss
She vied so fast, protesting oath on oath,
That in a twink she won me to her love.
O, you are novices! 'Tis a world to see
How tame, when men and women are alone,
A meacock wretch can make the curstest shrew.
Give me thy hand, Kate; I will unto Venice,
To buy apparel 'gainst the wedding-day.
Provide the feast, father, and bid the guests;
I will be sure my Katherine shall be fine.

BAPTISTA I know not what to say; but give me your hands.
God send you joy, Petruchio! 'Tis a match.

GREMIO and **TRANIO** Amen, say we; we will be witnesses.

PETRUCHIO Father and wife, and gentlemen, adieu.
I will to Venice; Sunday comes apace;
We will have rings and things, and fine array;
And kiss me, Kate; we will be married a Sunday.

*Exeunt **Petruchio** and **Katherine** severally.*

GLOSSARY

rail use abusive language, mock

'dainties are all Kates' a pun on 'cate' – meaning a cake or sweetmeat

moveable a piece of furniture

'if no gentleman, why then no arms' a reference to the coat of arms that a gentleman would be entitled to

jade a worn-out horse, or also a woman

swain a suitor or rustic lover

buzzard bird of prey

turtle turtle-dove

cox-comb a conceited showy person – a show-off

craven coward

crab crab apple

Dian the goddess Diana

'in your dumps' depressed, sulky

froward wayward, peevish, difficult

Grissel Patient Griselda, a character in an old tale

Lucrece a Roman wife, famous for her purity

meacock feeble, cowardly

'Then vail your stomachs' do homage, lower yourself

'for it is no boot' it is no use

Staging the Scene

 SET DESIGN

There have been innumerable different stagings of this play during its history, and it has proved the ideal 'star vehicle' for actors, from Ellen Terry and Henry Irving in 1867 to Richard Burton and Elizabeth Taylor in the 1967 film.

This scene takes place in Baptista's house in Padua. In deciding how to stage the scene, it is important to remember that Shakespeare's theatre used very little furniture and few props. Several strong details will be more effective than an over-elaborate attempt to suggest Renaissance Italy. A colourful hanging could suggest a rich tapestry and would place the scene in an interior space. Alternatively, with a carefully placed trellis, urn or balustrade the setting might indicate a courtyard or garden. A simple seat or bench, if necessary disguised by a piece of material or a shawl, will be useful to the actors.

A plain backdrop, with warm lighting, or a slide projection of a Mediterranean landscape, will help to create the sense of an Italian setting.

 MUSIC

If you decide to stage the scene in period, appropriate recorded Renaissance music would help to create an atmosphere before the scene starts. Live musicians, playing simple airs on guitar or recorder would add a great deal to the scene. If you are aiming for a more modern, lighthearted effect, you might play a selection from *Kiss Me Kate*, the musical based on *The Taming of the Shrew*.

 COSTUMES

Sometimes the play has been updated and performed in modern dress, or in very basic costumes. You may be able to hire or create authentic costumes of the period. Portraits, books of stage costume and historical sources will be helpful. Otherwise, dark trousers tucked into boots and a plain open-necked shirt will be adequate for Petruchio, perhaps with a short cloak. Kate could wear a long skirt with a low-necked, long-sleeved top and a scarf or shawl. The minor characters might wear cloaks, dark breeches or trousers and boots. To suggest his age, Baptista could wear a grey beard.

Elizabeth Taylor as Katherine in The Taming of the Shrew, *directed by Franco Zeffirelli (1967).*

Exploring the Scene

Aims

The activities in this section offer opportunities to:

English Framework Objective	Activity
(S&L13) Develop and compare different interpretations of the characters and their actions.	A, C, H
(S&L12) Use a range of drama techniques to explore a variety of issues, ideas and meanings	B, C, D, G
(R14) Analyse the language, form and dramatic impact of scenes	C
(W8) Write within the discipline of different forms	E, I
(R6) Recognise bias and objectivity	F
(R15) Extend understanding of literary heritage by relating the writer to his historical context and explaining his appeal over time	H, J
(S&L15) Write critical evaluations of performances seen or participated in	D

EXPLORING CHARACTERS

A. Character Sketches

Dramatists sometimes provide short character sketches of the people in their plays. Shakespeare tends to identify his characters only by their position in society or their relationship to other characters.

1. Write a brief character sketch, no more than six lines long, of Katherine as she appears in this scene. What is her attitude to Petruchio, and later to her father?

2. Write a brief description of Petruchio's appearance and personality.

3. What adjectives have you used to describe them both? Are some of the adjectives the same for both characters?

4. Make two columns and head one of them **KATE** and the other **PETRUCIO**.

   Put a list of all the names Petrucio calls Kate in one column and all names Kate calls Petrucio in the other column. Are any of these names positive?

   At one point in the scene, Katherine strikes Petruchio and he threatens to strike her back. What does this tell us about them both?

B. Improvisation

In pairs

1. *Organisation*: Work with a partner. One person takes on the role of either Kate or Petrucio. The other person is a close friend and confidante.

   Situation: You have decided to tell your friend about your recent encounter. Can you find anything good to say about your proposed marriage partner?

   Opening Line: **KATE/PETRUCHIO** I'm going to be married!

2. *Organisation*: Work in pairs. One person takes on the role of Baptista, Kate's father, and the other is Bianca, his youngest daughter.

   Situation: Baptista is greatly relieved to have found a husband for Kate. He tells Bianca about Petruchio's proposal and Kate's reaction to it. How does he convince himself, in spite of Kate's violent objections, that she really wants to marry Petruchio?

   Opening Line: **BAPTISTA** I think that underneath she really likes him...

DRAMATIC TECHNIQUES

C. Examining Style and Mood

7

1. Petruchio talks directly to the audience, and explains what his plan is for dealing with Kate. Playwrights often provide the audience with information that the characters don't possess. Can you find examples of this technique of direct address in the other scenes in this book?

cont...

2. Notice that the scene contains many one-line exchanges between Kate and Petruchio. How does Petruchio deal with Kate's quick tongue and ready wit? Does he always manage to keep to his plan of responding only with gentleness? Are there any hints in the scene that Kate is enjoying the battle of wits?

3. **Freeze Frame.** Pick out what you think is the **climax** or turning point of the scene. Remember that the most powerful instant might be a moment of stillness, a *realisation*, rather than an emotional or physical reaction. Is it possible to show this moment in a freeze frame?

In groups

4. **Hot-seating.** Kate falls silent at the end of this scene. Do you think that she has really accepted that her marriage to Petruchio is inevitable? To help you understand Kate's feelings or those of Petrucio during the scene you can use the technique of 'hot-seating'.

   Work in a small group. Take turns to adopt the role of either Katherine or Petruchio, and sit in the 'hot-seat', in front of the others in the group. As you are questioned by the others, you must try to answer honestly, from the point of view of the role you have adopted. The purpose of the exercise is to try to understand the character's real feelings and motives in the scene.

COMPARING TEXTS – PERIOD AND CULTURE

D. Theme for comparison: Arranged Marriages

Kate's father agrees to her marriage with Petruchio against her will. Several other plays by Shakespeare include situations where marriage partners are chosen by parents, including *A Midsummer Night's Dream* and *Romeo and Juliet*. For many centuries arranged marriages were accepted as the norm, and still occur today in some communities and cultures.

However, in *Twelfth Night* Shakespeare deals with the situation where two young women have no parents or brothers on hand to arrange their marriages and have to make the decisions alone. Viola has been cast onto the island of Illyria after a shipwreck and has to fend for herself, whilst Olivia, a noblewoman of Illyria, has lost both her parents and more recently her brother, and so has no-one to advise her on a marriage partner while being plagued with courtship requests on all sides.

1. Can you think of convincing arguments for arranged marriages?

2. Make a list of reasons why a parent might want to choose a particular partner for their child.

3. Write a short scene in which

   a a parent tries to persuade their son or daughter to marry someone they have chosen.

   Or

   b one person proposes to another and won't take no for an answer.

   Or

   c write a monologue either for a parent who has chosen a partner for their reluctant child, or a child who is being forced to consider marriage with a partner of the parent's choice.

   Decide whether the scene takes place in a contemporary setting, or if it will be more effective set in the past. Is one of the characters more sympathetic than the other? Are their arguments carefully balanced?

   Remember to:

   - provide details about the setting at the beginning of the scene,
   - include stage directions to help the actors in creating their characters.
   - give your characters names, and include details that will help convey their personalities and their motivation.

4. Present your scene to the rest of the group.

5. Watch the scenes presented by others in the group and evaluate the success of their efforts in creating characters and dialogue, an interesting setting and an effective plot.

6. Write a review of at least one of the scenes that were presented.

THEME FOR COMPARISON: WOMEN IN SOCIETY

E. Petruchio's Victory

In the last act, there is a wedding feast for the three couples, Hortensio, who has married a widow, Lucentio, who has married Bianca in secret, and Petruchio and Katherine. Petruchio makes a bet with Hortensio and Lucentio, which will be won by the husband whose wife is most obedient to him. Because of Katherine's reputation as a shrew, Petruchio seems certain to lose. To everyone's surprise, Katherine wins the bet for him with her final speech, in which she advises the other women to obey their husbands in everything.

> **KATE** Thy husband is thy lord, thy life, thy keeper,
> Thy head, thy sovereign, one that cares for thee,
> And for thy maintenance commits his body
> To painful labour both by sea and land,
> To watch the night in storms, the day in cold,
> Whilst thou liest warm at home, secure and safe,
> And craves no other tribute at thy hands
> But love, fair looks, and true obedience,
> Too little payment for so dear a debt.
> Such duty as the subject owes the prince,
> Even such a woman oweth to her husband,
> And when she is froward, peevish, sullen, sour,
> And not obedient to his honest will,
> What is she but a foul contending rebel,
> And graceless traitor to her loving lord?
> I am ashamed that women are so simple
> To offer war where they should kneel for peace,
> Or seek for rule, supremacy, and sway
> When they are bound to serve, love and obey.
> Why are our bodies soft, and weak, and smooth,
> Unapt to toil and trouble in the world,
> But that our soft conditions and our hearts
> Should well agree with our external parts?
> Come, come, you froward and unable worms,
> My mind hath been as big as one of yours,
> My heart as great, my reason haply more,
> To bandy word for word and frown for frown;
> But now I see our lances are but straws,
> Our strength as weak, our weakness past compare,
> That seeming to be most which we indeed least are.
> Then vail your stomachs, for it is no boot,
> And place your hands below your husband's foot,
> In token of which duty, if he please,
> My hand is ready, may it do him ease.

PETRUCHIO Why, there's a wench! Come on and kiss me, Kate.

F. Reviews

Many critics have commented on the play's ending.

....the last scene is altogether disgusting to modern sensibility. No man with any decency of feeling can sit it out without feeling extremely ashamed of the lord-of-creation moral implied in the wager and the speech put into the woman's own mouth.

George Bernard Shaw, 1897

..you can hardly refuse to shed a tear for the humiliation of Katherine...she stands for all time as a type of all the wrongs done to her much enduring sex.

E.K.Chambers, 1925

We are left at the end with the feeling that Katherine has at least enough spirit left to be a fit wife for Petruchio (who would have been driven into a premature grave by boredom with Bianca). No doubt they will spar; but life would not be worth living to either of then unless they did; and after some excellent and spirited fooling we can see them to bed with as confident hope of their being happy ever after...

M.R.Ridley, 1937

Katherine is a woman striving for her existence in a world where she is a...decoy to be bid for against her sister's higher market value, so she opts out by becoming unmanageable. She has the uncommon good fortune to find Petruchio who is man enough to know what he wants and how to get it. He wants her spirit and her energy because he wants a wife worth keeping.

Germaine Greer, 1970

Why would a modern theatre company want to resurrect Shakespeare's most cringe-worthy, inflammatory play? Do they not realise that half their audience will be women and will most likely be incensed or at least affronted by the submission of the spiky Kate by such cruel means? What place has the play in our society now – by modern tastes is it still even a comedy?

Review on the Internet of a recent production, 2001

But in earlier times some commentators felt differently.

…the crabbed shrew is forced to resign her absurd pretensions and is completely cured by the merry device of her husband, who pretends to be possessed by a similar but greater petulance; and, though put to shame by the distorted image of her own perversity, she is restored to the modest position which naturally becomes her sex.

Hermann Ulrici, 1839

Katherine's harangue to her Sister and the Widow on the Duty of Wives to their Husbands, if the Ladies would read it with a little Regard, would be of mighty Use in this Age.

Charles Gildon, 1710

Some of these critics seem to feel that Petruchio and Katherine are well suited to each other and will be happy together.

1. Which critics think this and what reasons do they give?

2. Do you agree with any of the opinions expressed above? Why?

3. Do any of these opinions surprise you?

G. Critics' Forum

Bring the discussion to life by asking some of the group to take on the roles of these critics. Discuss the ages and appearance of these writers, and the way they might speak. The 'critics' then take turns to present their views to the class, and try to defend their opinions.

H. Discussion

Many modern productions of the play have difficulty with this speech, which seems so different from Kate's previous behaviour. She seems to be saying that women should be totally subservient to their husbands. Modern audiences are likely to have problems with this view.

1. Do you think that Kate really believes what she is saying?

2. Is there a conspiracy between Kate and Petruchio to win the bet?

3. What other interpretations might there be to explain her surprising speech?

4. Do you agree with anything that she says?

5. Why do you think that the play is still popular, in spite of its controversial ending?

6. Do you agree that Kate's speech of submission is offensive to women?

I. Writing

1. Imagine that Kate has become a time-traveller and arrived in modern Britain. Write her a letter of advice, from a modern viewpoint, explaining the position of women in the 21st century. You might begin –

> Dear Kate,
>
> You'll find things are very different for women today. For example....

Don't forget to include:

- details of the opportunities for women in education
- the professions that are open to them
- the position of women within the family
- changes in the relationships between men and women
- different views of marriage

cont...

H

Or:

2. Write a story or a scene in which someone seems to undergo a real change of character or opinion. As the central character, choose someone with strong opinions, either about particular people, or about some aspect of the modern world.

- What might cause this person to alter his or her views?
- Will it be because of someone the main character encounters?
- Has a particular incident or event occurred that changes this person's attitude or behaviour?

3. Read your letter or story aloud, or present your scene to the rest of the class.

J. Research

Look at the glossary. How many of these words are familiar to you?

Make a list of any other words in the scene whose meaning is not clear and look them up in a dictionary.

Use a thesaurus to find a word of a similar meaning and replace it in the scene. Is it as effective as the original?

Search the Internet for information about Shakespeare and his time, and *The Taming of the Shrew*. Compile a portfolio that includes all you research.

The play formed the basis for *Kiss Me Kate*, a highly successful musical and film. Find a video of the musical and compare the presentation of this scene to Shakespeare's original.

Hobson's Choice

Harold Brighouse

HAROLD BRIGHOUSE

Harold Brighouse was born near Salford in Lancashire in 1882. At the age of 17 he began working in the cotton industry as a clerk in a shipping merchant's warehouse. He greatly enjoyed the theatre, but after seeing a bad production of a poor play decided that he could do better himself. Although his first effort at playwriting was rejected, he persevered, and by 1911 he had written three successful plays, including the extremely popular *Lonesome-Like* which ran for 3000 performances.

His career now began to take off. Three more plays quickly followed dealing with subjects as diverse as football and political corruption. In 1915, the year in which *Hobson's Choice* was first produced, he left the cotton trade and was recognised as a successful author.

Brighouse was associated with a group of local writers based around the Gaiety Theatre in Manchester who became known as the 'Manchester school'. The Gaiety was one of the first Repertory Theatres to be founded in England. In these theatres, different plays were presented for a short run of performances but kept in the company's repertoire of plays and performed again later in the season. Unlike the usual practice of employing a few star performers and a new supporting cast for each play, the Repertory Theatres made use of a permanent group of actors who appeared in all of the different plays that were presented each season. They concentrated on new plays featuring realistic characters and reflecting important issues of the time. The English Stage Society at the Court Theatre in London had pioneered this method of working under its influential director, Harley Granville Barker. Plays were staged there by such controversial authors as George Bernard Shaw and Henrik Ibsen. Brighouse's *Dealing in Futures* about an attempt to conceal the poisoning of workers in a chemical factory, bears some similarity to Ibsen's *An Enemy of the People*, in which prominent members of a community attempt to hush up an infection in the local water supply.

Hobson's Choice was written in 1914, soon after the outbreak of the First World War. Brighouse's friend and fellow playwright Stanley Houghton had recently died, and as a distraction from his grief he turned his hand to writing comedy. After being rejected by London theatres, the play opened in New York in 1916 and was a major success. It soon transferred to London, received ecstatic reviews and ran for 246 performances.

Hobson's Choice was Brighouse's most successful play, and made him internationally famous. It has been regularly produced over the last 85 years and was filmed in 1954. Brighouse continued writing, and by the time of his death in 1958 had written 15 full-length plays, and eight novels.

SUMMARY OF THE PLOT

Although it was written in 1914, the play is set in 1880, in Hobson's Boot Shop in Salford. The proprietor, Henry Horatio Hobson, rules his business and his family with a rod of iron. He is particularly incensed at what he calls the "uppishness" of his two youngest daughters, who will insist on having boyfriends and dressing in the latest fashions. His eldest daughter Maggie, he believes, is well and truly "on the shelf at the age of thirty". He takes comfort in the fact that she will remain with, him to continue organizing the day-to-day running of the shop. However, Maggie has other ideas having set her sights on marrying the bootmaker, Will Mossop. In spite of her family's opposition, she and Will set up a home and workshop in two basement rooms. By the start of the fourth act, the fortunes of the major characters have been completely transformed. Maggie and Will have by now established a successful shop of their own and Hobson has lost most of his business to them. Hobson is faced with the dilemma of seeing his business collapse or becoming the sleeping partner in the new firm of Mossop and Hobson with Willy and Maggie taking over his premises. He is faced with an option which he cannot refuse – the proverbial "Hobson's choice".

THE SCENE IN CONTEXT

In this scene we see Maggie having realised that the success of the business depends not just on her skill with customers but on the skill of the talented but self-effacing bootmaker, Will Mossop. She resolves to marry him, and the comedy of this proposal scene comes from the contrast between her assertiveness and his slowly dawning realisation of her intentions and reluctance to go along with them. Maggie's decision to marry Will Mossop horrifies her sisters and astounds her father.

Hobson's Choice

By

Harold Brighouse

CAST LIST

MAGGIE HOBSON, eldest daughter of Henry Hobson, owner of
    Hobson's Boot Shop
WILL MOSSOP, bootmaker employed by Hobson
ADA FIGGINS, daughter of Will Mossop's landlady, who believes
    herself to be engaged to Will
ALICE HOBSON, Hobson's second daughter, aged twenty-three
VICKEY HOBSON, Hobson's youngest daughter, aged twenty-one
HENRY HORATIO HOBSON, owner of Hobson's Boot Shop, fifty-five
    years old

ACT ONE

*The interior of Hobson's shoe shop. There is a trapdoor leading to the cellar
in the centre of the floor.*

47   *Maggie raises the trap.*

MAGGIE Willie, come here.

Willie appears and stops half-way up.

WILLIE Yes, Miss Maggie!

MAGGIE Come up and put the trap down. I want to talk to you.

He comes, reluctantly.

WILLIE We're very busy in the cellar.

MAGGIE Show me your hands, Willie.

WILLIE They're dirty. *(he holds them out, hesitatingly)*

MAGGIE Yes, they're dirty, but they're clever. They can shape leather like no man's that ever came into the shop. Who taught you, Willie?

WILLIE Why, Miss Maggie, I learnt my trade here.

MAGGIE Hobson's never taught you to make boots the way you do.

WILLIE I've had no other teacher.

MAGGIE And needed none. You're a natural genius at making boots. It's a pity you're a natural fool at all else.

WILLIE I'm not much good at owt but leather, and that's a fact.

MAGGIE When are you going to leave Hobson's?

WILLIE Leave Hobson's? I – I thought I gave satisfaction.

MAGGIE Don't you want to leave?

WILLIE Not me. I've been at Hobson's all my life, and I'm not for leaving till I'm made.

MAGGIE I said you were a fool.

WILLIE Then I'm a loyal fool.

MAGGIE Don't you want to get on, Will Mossop? You heard what Mrs. Hepworth said. You know the wages you get and you know the wages a bootmaker like you could get in one of the big shops in Manchester.

WILLIE Nay, I'd be feared to go in them fine places.

MAGGIE What keeps you here? Is it – the people?

WILLIE I dunno what it is. I'm used to being here.

MAGGIE Do you know what keeps this business on its legs? Two things: one's the good boots you make that sell themselves, the other's the bad boots other people make and I sell. We're a pair, Will Mossop.

WILLIE You're a wonder in the shop, Miss Maggie.

MAGGIE And you're a marvel in the workshop. Well?

WILLIE Well, what?

MAGGIE It seems to me to point one way.

WILLIE What way is that?

MAGGIE You're leaving me to do the work, my lad.

WILLIE I'll be getting back to my stool, Miss Maggie.

MAGGIE You'll go back when I've done with you. I've watched you for a long time, and everything I've seen, I've liked. I think you'll do for me.

WILLIE What way, Miss Maggie?

MAGGIE Will Mossop, you're my man. Six months I've counted on you, and it's got to come out some time.

WILLIE But I never —

MAGGIE I know you never, or it'd not be left to me to do the job like this.

WILLIE I'll – I'll sit down. *(he sits in armchair, mopping his brow)* I'm feeling queer-like. What dost want me for?

MAGGIE To invest in. You're a business idea in the shape of a man.

WILLIE I've got no head for business at all.

MAGGIE But I have. My brain and your hands will make a working partnership.

WILLIE *getting up, relieved* Partnership! Oh, that's a different thing. I thought you were axing me to wed you.

MAGGIE I am.

WILLIE Well, by gum! And you the master's daughter.

MAGGIE Maybe that's why, Will Mossop. Maybe I've had enough of Father, and you're as different from him as any man I know.

WILLIE It's a bit awkward-like.

MAGGIE And you don't help me any, lad. What's awkward about it?

WILLIE You talking to me like this.

MAGGIE I'll tell you something, Will. It's a poor sort of woman who'll stay lazy when she sees her best chance slipping from her. A Salford life's too near the bone to lose things through the fear of speaking out.

WILLIE I'm you're best chance?

MAGGIE You are that, Will.

WILLIE Well, by gum! I never thought of this.

MAGGIE Think of it now.

WILLIE I am doing. Only the blow's a bit too sudden to think very clear. I've a great respect for you, Miss Maggie. You're a shapely body and you're a masterpiece at selling in the shop, but when it comes to marrying, I'm bound to tell you that I'm none in love with you.

MAGGIE Wait till you're asked. I want your hand in mine and your word for it that you'll go through life with me for the best we can get out of it.

WILLIE We'd not get much without there's love between us, lass.

MAGGIE I've got the love all right.

WILLIE Well, I've not, and that's honest.

MAGGIE We'll get along without.

WILLIE You're desperate set on this. It's a puzzle to me all ways. What'd your father say?

MAGGIE He'll say a lot and he can say it. It'll make no difference to me.

WILLIE Much better not upset him. It's not worthwhile.

MAGGIE I'm judge of that. You're going to wed me, Will.

WILLIE Oh nay, I'm not. Really I can't do that, Maggie. I can see that I'm disturbing your arrangements like, but I'll be obliged if you'll put this notion from you.

MAGGIE When I make arrangements, my lad, they're not made for upsetting.

WILLIE What makes it so desperate awkward is that I'm tokened.

MAGGIE You're what?

WILLIE I'm tokened to Ada Figgins.

MAGGIE Then you'll get loose and quick. Who's Ada Figgins? Do I know her?

WILLIE I'm the lodger at her mother's.

MAGGIE The scheming hussy. It's not that sandy girl who brings your dinner?

WILLIE She's golden-haired, is Ada. Aye, she'll be here soon.

MAGGIE And so shall I. I'll talk to Ada. I've seen her and I know the breed. Ada's the helpless sort.

WILLIE She needs protecting.

MAGGIE That's how she got you, was it? Yes, I can see her clinging round your neck until you fancied you were strong. But I'll tell you this, my lad, it's a desperate poor kind of a woman that'll look for protection to the likes of you.

WILLIE Ada does.

MAGGIE And that gives me the weight of her. She's born to meekness, Ada is. You wed her and you'll be an eighteen-shilling-a-week bootmaker all the days of your life. You'll be a slave, and a contented slave.

WILLIE I'm not ambitious that I know of.

MAGGIE No, but you're going to be. I'll see to that. I've got my work cut out, but there's the makings of a man about you.

WILLIE I wish you'd leave me alone.

MAGGIE So does the fly when the spider catches him. You're my man, Willie Mossop.

WILLIE Aye, so you say. Ada would tell another story, though.

*Ada Figgins enters from street. She is not ridiculous, but a weak, poor-blooded, poor-spirited girl of twenty, in clogs and shawl, with **Willie's** dinner in a basin carried in a blue handkerchief. She crosses to him and gives him the basin.*

ADA There's your dinner, Will.

WILLIE Thank you, Ada. *(she turns to go and finds **Maggie** in her way)*

MAGGIE I want a word with you. You're treading on my foot, young woman.

ADA Me, Miss 'Obson? *(she looks stupidly at **Maggie's** feet)*

MAGGIE What's this with you and him?

ADA *gushing* Oh, Miss 'Obson, it's good of you to take notice like that.

WILLIE Ada, she –

MAGGIE You hold your hush. This is for me and her to settle. Take a fair look at him, Ada.

ADA At Will?

MAGGIE Not much for two women to fall out over, is there?

ADA Maybe he's not much to look at, but you should hear him play.

MAGGIE Play? Are you a musician, Will?

WILLIE I play the Jew's harp.

MAGGIE That's what you see in him, is it? A gawky fellow that plays the Jew's harp?

ADA I see the lad I love, Miss 'Obson.

MAGGIE It's a funny thing, but I can say the same.

ADA You!

WILLIE That's what I've been trying to tell you, Ada, and – and, by gum, she'll have me from you if you don't be careful.

MAGGIE So we're quits so far, Ada.

ADA You'll pardon me. You've spoke too late. Will and me's tokened.

MAGGIE That's the past. It's the future that I'm looking to. What's your idea for that?

ADA You mind your own business, Miss 'Obson. Will Mossop's no concern of thine.

WILLIE That's what I try to tell her myself, only she will have it it's no use.

MAGGIE Not an atom. I've asked for your idea of Willie's future. If it's a likelier one than mine, I'll give you best and you can have the lad.

ADA I'm trusting him to make the future right.

MAGGIE It's as bad as I thought it was. Willie, you wed me.

ADA *weakly* It's daylight robbery.

WILLIE Aren't you going to put up a better fight for me than that, Ada? You're fair giving me to her.

MAGGIE Will Mossop, you take your orders from me in this shop. I've told you you'll wed me.

WILLIE Seems like there's no escape.

ADA Wait till I get you to home, my lad. I'll set my mother on to you.

MAGGIE Oh, so it's her mother made this match!

WILLIE She had above a bit to do with it.

48

MAGGIE I've got no mother, Will.

WILLIE You need none, neither.

MAGGIE Well, can I sell you a pair of clogs, Miss Figgins?

ADA No, nor anything else.

MAGGIE Then you've no business here, have you?

ADA Will, are you going to see me ordered out?

WILLIE It's her shop, Ada.

ADA You mean I'm to go like this?

WILLIE She means it.

ADA It's cruel hard.

MAGGIE When it comes to a parting, it's best to part sudden and no whimpering about it.

ADA I'm not whimpering and I'm not parting either. But he'll whimper tonight when my mother sets about him. *(she opens door)*

MAGGIE That'll do.

ADA Will Mossop, I'm telling you, you'll come home tonight to a thick ear. *(she goes)*

WILLIE I'd really rather wed Ada, Maggie, if it's all the same to you.

MAGGIE Why? Because of her mother?

WILLIE She's a terrible rough side to her tongue, has Mrs. Figgins.

MAGGIE Are you afraid of her?

WILLIE *hesitates* Yes.

MAGGIE You needn't be.

WILLIE Yes, but you don't know her. She jaw me till I'm black in the face when I go home tonight.

MAGGIE You won't go home tonight.

WILLIE Not go!

MAGGIE You've done with lodging there. You'll go to Tubby Wadlow's when you knock off work, and Tubby'll go round to Mrs. Figgins for your things.

WILLIE And I'm not to go back there never no more?

MAGGIE No.

WILLIE It's like a happy dream. Eh, Maggie, you do manage things.

MAGGIE And while Tubby's there you can go round and see about putting up the banns for us two.

WILLIE Banns! Oh, I'm hardly used to the idea yet.

MAGGIE You'll have three weeks to get used to it in. Now you can kiss me, Will.

WILLIE That's forcing things a bit, and all. It's like saying I agree to everything, a kiss is.

MAGGIE Yes.

WILLIE And I don't agree yet. I'm –

MAGGIE Come along. (*Alice and then Vickey, enter from the living apartments*) Do what I tell you, Will.

WILL Now? With them here?

MAGGIE Yes.

WILL *pause* I couldn't. (*he dives for trap, runs down, and closes it*)

ALICE What's the matter with Will?

MAGGIE He's a bit upset because I've told him he's to marry me. Is dinner cooking nicely?

ALICE You're going to marry Willie Mossop? Willie Mossop!

VICKEY You've kept it very quiet, Maggie.

MAGGIE You know about it pretty near as soon as Willie does himself.

VICKEY Well, I don't know!

ALICE I know, and if you're afraid to speak your thoughts, I'm not. Look here, Maggie, what you do touches us, and you're mistaken if you think I'll own Willie Mossop for my brother-in-law.

MAGGIE Is there supposed to be some disgrace in him?

ALICE You ask Father if there's some disgrace. And look at me. I'd hopes of Albert Prosser till this happened.

MAGGIE You'll marry Albert Prosser when he's able, and that'll be when he starts spending less on laundry bills and hair-cream.

Hobson enters from the streets.

HOBSON Well, what about that dinner?

MAGGIE It'll be ready in ten minutes.

HOBSON You said one o'clock.

MAGGIE Yes, Father. One for half-past. If you'll wash your hands it'll be ready as soon as you are.

HOBSON I won't wash my hands. I don't hold with such finicking ways, and well you know it.

VICKEY Father, have you heard the news about our Maggie?

HOBSON News? There is no news. It's the same old tale. Uppishness. You'd keep a starving man from the meat he earns in the sweat of his brow, would you? I'll put you in your places. I'll –

MAGGIE Don't lose your temper, Father. You'll maybe need it soon when Vickey speaks.

HOBSON What's Vickey been doing?

VICKEY Nothing. It's about Will Mossop, Father.

HOBSON Will?

ALICE Yes. What's your opinion of Will?

HOBSON A decent lad. I've nowt against him that I know of.

ALICE Would you like him in the family?

HOBSON Whose family?

VICKEY Yours.

MAGGIE I'm going to marry Willie, Father. That's what all the fuss is about.

HOBSON Marry – you – Mossop?

MAGGIE You thought me past the marrying age. I'm not. That's all.

HOBSON Didn't you hear me say I'd do the choosing when it came to a question of husbands?

MAGGIE You said I was too old to get a husband.

HOBSON You are. You all are.

VICKEY Father!

HOBSON And if you're not, it makes no matter. I'll have no husbands here.

ALICE But you said –

HOBSON I've changed my mind. I've learned some things since then. There's a lot too much expected of a father nowadays. There'll be no weddings here.

ALICE Oh, Father!

HOBSON Go and get my dinner served and talk less. Go on now. I'm not in right temper to be crossed.

*He drives **Alice** and **Vickey** before him. They go out protesting loudly. But **Maggie** stands in his way as he follows and she closes the door. She looks at him from the stair.*

MAGGIE You and I'll be straight with one another, Father. I'm not a fool and you're not a fool, and things may as well be put in their places as left untidy.

HOBSON I tell you my mind's made up. You can't have Willie Mossop. Why, lass, his father was a workhouse brat. A come-by-chance.

MAGGIE It's news to me we're snobs in Salford. I have Willie Mossop. I've to settle my life's course, and a good course too, so think on.

HOBSON I'd be the laughing-stock of the place if I allowed it. I won't have it, Maggie. It's hardly decent at your time of life.

MAGGIE I'm thirty and I'm marrying Willie Mossop. And now I'll tell you my terms.

HOBSON You're in a nice position to state terms, my lass.

MAGGIE You will pay my man, Will Mossop, the same wages as before. And as for me, I've given you the better part of twenty years of work without wages. I'll work eight hours a day in future, and you will pay me fifteen shillings by the week.

HOBSON Do you think I'm made of brass?

MAGGIE You'll soon be made of less than you are if you let Willie go. And if Willie goes, I go. That's what you've got to face.

HOBSON I might face it, Maggie. Shop hands are cheap.

MAGGIE Cheap ones are cheap. The sort you'd have to watch all day, and you'd feel happy helping them to tie up parcels and sell laces with Tudsbury and Heeler and Minns supping their ale without you. I'm value to you, so's my man; and you can boast it at the Moonraker's that your daughter Maggie's made the strangest, finest match a woman's made this fifty year. And you can put your hand in your pocket and do what I propose.

HOBSON I'll show you what I propose, Maggie. *(he lifts trap and calls)* Will Mossop! *(he places hat on counter and unbuckles belt)* I cannot leather you, my lass. You're female and exempt, but I can leather him. Come up, Will Mossop. (***Will** comes up trap and closes it)* You've taken up with my Maggie, I hear. *(he conceals strap)*

WILLIE Nay, I've not. She's done the taking up.

HOBSON Well, Willie, either way, you've fallen on misfortune. Love's led you astray, and I feel bound to put you right. *(shows strap)*

WILLIE Maggie, what's this?

MAGGIE I'm watching you, my lad.

HOBSON Mind, Willie, you can keep your job. I don't bear malice, but we must beat the love from your body, and every morning you come here to work with love still sitting in you, you'll get a leathering.

WILLIE You'll not beat love in me. You're making a great mistake, Mr. Hobson, and –

HOBSON You'll put aside your weakness for my Maggie if you've a liking for a sound skin. You'll waste a gradely lot of brass at chemist's if I am at you for a week with this. *(he swings the strap)*

WILLIE I'm none wanting thy Maggie, it's her that's after me, but I'll tell you this, Mr. Hobson – if you touch me with that belt, I'll take her quick , aye, and stick to her like glue.

HOBSON There's nobbut one answer to that kind of talk, my lad.

*He strikes with belt. **Maggie** shrinks.*

WILLIE And I've nobbut one answer back. Maggie, I've none kissed you yet. I shirked before. But, by gum, I'll kiss you now – *(he kisses her quickly, with temper, not with passion, as quickly leaves her, to face **Hobson**)* – and take you and hold you. And if Mr. Hobson raises up that strap again, I'll do more. I'll walk straight out of shop with thee and us two'll set up for ourselves.

MAGGIE Willie! I knew you had it in you, lad.

*She puts her arm round his neck. He is quite unresponsive. His hands fall limply to his sides. **Hobson** stands in amazed indecision.*

End of Act One

GLOSSARY

Owt anything

Tokened engaged, betrothed

I'll give you best I'll give in to you, give you victory

She'll jaw me she'll tell me off

Putting the banns up posting the announcement of the marriage

Staging the Scene

 ## SET DESIGN

The setting for this scene is the interior of Hobson's Boot Shop in Chapel Street, Salford. In the published script, the setting is very naturalistic and detailed:

> The shop-windows and entrance from the street occupy the right side. Opposite is the counter, with exhibits of boots and slippers, behind which the wall is filled with racks containing boot-boxes. Cane chairs in front of counter. A door centre leads up two stairs to the house. In the corner of the stage is a trap door leading to the cellar. There are no elaborate fittings. Gas-brackets in the windows and walls.

The setting you choose may be very detailed or extremely simple, depending on your intentions, and the available performance space and resources. If you can't arrange a trap door in your performance space, you will need to remove the reference to it in the script, or find some other way of representing Will's workroom. For example, you might place the workroom on a lower level than the shop. Will could be seated at a workbench or on a stool, before he is summoned by Maggie. But however simple the set, you will need to include a chair, and to indicate an entrance from the street, as well as the access to the workplace, or cellar, for Willie.

In designing and furnishing your set, you'll need to consider the following:

■ How will you indicate that this is Hobson's Boot Shop?

■ How many props will you need to include?

■ What sort of atmosphere do you want to convey?

COSTUMES

It should be relatively easy to use costumes to convey a sense of the period in which the play is set – the 1880s. Maggie's clothes should be plain and business-like – perhaps a long black or grey skirt, with a high-necked, long-sleeved blouse. This could be the same colour as her skirt, or white. Willie should wear shabby trousers, a collarless shirt and a large apron. Ada's dress will be plainer and less tidy than Maggie's. She will probably wear a shawl. Maggie's sisters' dresses will be more fashionable and colourful. You might add bright shawls to basic long skirts and blouses. Hobson will need a dark suit, a waistcoat, perhaps with a gold watch chain, and a white shirt with a high collar and tie.

Brenda De Banzie and John Mills in the 1954 film production of Hobson's Choice, *directed by David Lean.*

LIGHTING AND SOUND EFFECTS

The naturalistic nature of the scene does not require much in the way of lighting and sound effects, but skilful lighting will greatly enhance the effect of the scene. You could use carefully positioned lights to suggest the daylight outside the shop window, and lamp light streaming from the trap door or entrance to the workshop. Sound effects could include the tapping of the other bootmakers in the workroom. Sounds of horse drawn vehicles and the feet of passers-by from the street will add to the feeling of another age. If you don't want to use pre-recorded effects, make a sound tape, using people in your group to create the sound of footsteps and horses' hooves.

Exploring the Scene

Aims
The following activities will help you to:

English Framework Objective	Activity
(S&L12) Use a range of drama techniques to explore issues, ideas and meanings	C, E, F H, K, N
(R2) Synthesise information from a range of sources	M
(R14) Analyse the language, form and dramatic impact of the scene	D, F
(R12) Analyse and discuss the use of rhetorical devices in the text	J, M
(S&L10) Contribute to the organisation of group activity	C, E, F H, K, N
(S&L5) Compare different points of view, identifying and evaluating differences and similarities	B
(R7) Compare the presentation of ideas, values or emotions in related or contrasting texts	M
(W4) Choose, use and evaluate a range of presentational devices	L

EXPLORING CHARACTERS

A. Maggie

The playwright does not provide any physical description of Maggie, although Willie calls her 'a comely body'. Throughout the play she is contrasted with her two pretty, flighty sisters. Earlier in the play, Hobson, Maggie's father, is considering husbands for the younger girls. He brutally dismisses the idea of a husband for Maggie.

HOBSON If you want the brutal truth, you're past the marrying age. You're a proper old maid, Maggie, if ever there was one.

MAGGIE I'm thirty.

HOBSON Aye, thirty and shelved. Well, all the women can't get husbands.

It seems that this is one of the reasons that Maggie is so determined to show her father that she can find a husband.

What other reasons for marrying Will Mossop does Maggie mention in the scene?

B. Discussion

Maggie claims that she loves Will. Do you believe her?

- Are there any suggestions to support her claim in the text?
- Was Maggie right to propose to Willie, in spite of his reluctance?
- Do you admire Maggie's behaviour?
- What is her opinion of Willie?
- Do you agree with her?
- What is Maggie's opinion of Ada?
- How is Willie's view of Ada different?
- How do Vickey and Alice respond to Maggie?

If you are acting the part of Maggie you will face a number of challenges. Maggie is very business-like and determined in her dealings with Willie, Ada, and her family and this may make her seem rather unpleasant. The scene will be less effective if Maggie loses the sympathy of the audience. How will you convey that she may have a softer side to her character?

C. Improvisation

In pairs

Her father values Maggie for her skills in the shop. Will describes her as a 'masterpiece' at selling in the shop. She claims that she is even able to sell bad boots. *cont...*

> **1.** *Organisation*: Work with a partner. One of you plays Maggie and the other is a customer.
>
> *Situation*: Maggie is trying to persuade the reluctant customer to buy a pair of unsuitable boots or shoes.
>
> *Opening Line*: **MAGGIE** Now these really suit you.

D. Will

Brighouse describes Willie Mossop in some detail, even providing information about his childhood.

> *He is a lanky fellow, about thirty, not naturally stupid but stunted mentally by a brutalized childhood. He is the raw material of a charming man, but, at present, it requires a very keen eye to detect his potentialities.*

If you are playing the part of Willie, all your movement and gestures will help to convey your lowly social status in relation to Maggie. Remember that you spend your working life in a cellar, bent over the boots you are making. It will also be important to consider some of the following questions:

- What is Willie's attitude to Maggie before she proposes to him?
- How does his attitude to her change during and after the proposal?
- Do you get any indication from his behaviour or speech during the scene that Willie has a sense of humour and is not completely down-trodden?
- Why does Willie allow Maggie to send Ada away?
- What does this tell us about his character?
- How does our view of Will change after his confrontation with Hobson?

E. Improvisation

In pairs

1. *Organisation*: Work with a partner. One of you plays Will, and the other is Tubby Wadlow, who also works at Hobson's Boot Shop.

Situation: Will confides in Tubby what has happened between him and Maggie.

Opening Line: **WILL** I've just been talking to Miss Maggie.

F. Thought-tracking

In groups

There are several ways of using the technique of **thought-tracking** to clarify the relationship between Will and Maggie during this scene. Try these two:

1. Ask two people to act the scene, watched by the others in the group. At any point in the scene, the spectators can stop the actors and ask them to reveal their real thoughts at that moment.

2. Work in a group of four. Choose the first three pages of script. Two of those in the group take on the parts of Will and Maggie and the other two represent what is going on in their minds as they speak their lines. Each time Will and Maggie speak a line of dialogue where their thoughts might differ from what they actually say, stop the action. At this point we hear their real thoughts and feelings, spoken aloud by the two others in the group. Sometimes these thoughts may echo the dialogue, sometimes their thoughts may emphasise or contradict what we hear them say.

28

G. Ada

This is how the playwright describes Ada:

She is not ridiculous, but a weak, poor-blooded, poor-spirited girl of twenty, in clogs and shawl.

- What do you think it is about Ada that attracted Will to her?
- Do you think that Ada really loves Will?
- How would you describe her feelings for him?
- Do you feel any sympathy for Ada?
- What are the problems an actor might face in playing the part of Ada?

H. Improvisation

34

Maggie suggests that Ada and Will have become engaged because of her mother's interference. Can you include this suggestion in your scene?

1. *Organisation*: Work in a group of two or three. One of you plays Will, and the others are Ada and her mother, Mrs Figgins.

    Situation: During the scene Will finds that he has become engaged to Ada.

    Opening Line: **ADA** Will, I love hearing you play.

2. *Organisation*: Work with a partner. One of you plays Ada and the other is Ada's Mother.

    Situation: Ada returns home and breaks the news to her mother that Willie is now engaged to Maggie Hobson.

    Opening Line: **MRS FIGGINS** What's the matter, Ada?

I. Discussion

■ Do you find Maggie's proposal to Will amusing? Pick out any moments in the scene that strike you as funny.

■ Should women take the initiative in proposing?

■ Is it right to get married if there are no romantic feelings between the partners?

■ Do you think that Maggie and Will have a chance of happiness?

■ Is there a best age for getting married?

J. Hobson

The playwright describes Hobson as "successful, coarse, florid and a parent of the period." Although he only appears at the end of the scene, the behaviour of all the other characters is affected by Hobson's domineering personality. He is the typical Victorian father, who expects unquestioning obedience from his family.

1. Find examples of Hobson's unfairness to his daughters and to Will in the scene.

2. What clues does the scene give us about Hobson's values, attitudes and lifestyle?

3. What reasons does he offer for objecting to Will as a partner for Maggie?

4. How does Maggie try to manage her father? How successful are her efforts?

5. What criteria do you think Hobson might use in choosing husbands for his daughters?

6. Compare Hobson to the other parents who appear in these extracts. Which parent does he have most in common with?

7. What problems might a young actor face in playing the part of Hobson?

K. Forum Theatre

In this approach, originally developed by Augusto Boal, an improvised scene is presented to the rest of the group. At any point the actors or observers can stop the action to ask for help in the improvisation or to make suggestions about its development. The observers, or 'spect-actors', as Boal calls them, can step in and add a role, or take over an existing role.

In groups

Organisation: Work in a small group. Look again at the section of the scene where Hobson confronts his daughters. One person plays Hobson and the others take on the roles of his daughters.

Opening Line: **HOBSON** I'll have no husbands here.

The attitudes of Hobson and his daughters to the prospect of marriage will be very different. What arguments can the girls use to convince their father that if they get married he will benefit from the change?

Present your scene to the rest of the class. At any point those watching can interrupt the scene to suggest dialogue, take over a role or join in the improvisation in an appropriate role.

38

L. Writing

H

1. Make a list of adjectives that describe Maggie. How many of them are positive and how many are negative?

2. Repeat the exercise for Will, Ada and Hobson

3. Write a letter in which Maggie explains to her father the step she has taken and puts forward her terms.

4. Write an entry in Maggie's diary, on the night before she proposes to Will that reveals her feelings about him, and the reasons for her decision to marry him.

5. Write a monologue for (a) Willie and (b) Maggie, in which they explain to their grandchildren how they came to marry.

COMPARING TEXTS – CULTURE, PERIOD AND STYLE

M. Themes for comparison: Marriage and the Position of Women in Society

Both *Hobson's Choice* and *A Taste of Honey* are set in Salford, although they are separated in time by more than sixty years. Read both scenes and see if you can discover any similarities between the characters. In addition, compare both scenes to the scene from *The Taming of the Shrew* and also the play *Billy Liar* by Waterhouse and Hall.

- What clues can you find to give you information about the attitudes and values of the characters?

- How have relationships between parents and children altered?

- How have people's views changed about marriage, and the appropriate age for women to get married?

- Both playwrights aimed to give a realistic picture of life and relationships. Which do you think is the most successful?

- How do you think the characters in these scenes would fit into life today?

N. Improvisation

In groups

Use this exercise to explore similarities and contrasts among the parents represented in this selection of scenes. How will the different times and cultures from which they come affect their attitudes to their daughters?

1. *Organisation*: Work in a group of three or four. The scene includes Will and/or Maggie. The other characters are Jo and her mother Helen.

   Situation: Jo is complaining about her mother's upcoming marriage.

   Opening Line: **JO** What does she want to get married for, at her age?

2. *Organisation*: Work with a partner. One of you is Ada and the other is Jo.

   Situation: Jo and Ada meet. They begin to compare the behaviour and characters of their mothers.

   Opening Line: **ADA** My mother wants me to get married.

3. *Organisation*: Work in a small group. Each person takes on the role of either Baptista, Hobson or Helen.

   Situation: The group meets in a situation where they are forced to stay with each other, for example a railway carriage. They begin to discuss the duties and difficulties of parenthood.

   Opening line: **HOBSON** Daughters are nothing but trouble!

The Caucasian Chalk Circle

Bertolt Brecht

BERTOLT BRECHT

Bertolt Brecht was born in Germany in 1898. He was a sickly child and he suffered a heart attack at the age of twelve. He began writing while he was still in school and by the time he was sixteen he had written his first play. The First World War broke out in 1914. Because of his poor health he avoided any direct experience of the horrors of the trenches, but he saw the terrible results of war working as a medical orderly in an emergency hospital. He was released from service after openly expressing his lack of conviction for the war.

He moved first to Munich and then to Berlin, where he soon found work as a theatre critic. In 1922 his play *Drums in the Night* was performed, followed by *In the Jungle of the Cities* and *Baal*. He achieved real success with *The Threepenny Opera*, a new version of *The Beggar's Opera* with music by Kurt Weill. In 1929 he married the communist actress Helene Wiegel, by whom he had two children after divorcing his first wife, whom he had married in 1924.

By 1933 the Nazis were taking power in Germany, and they revoked Brecht's German citizenship in 1935. Brecht's support for Communism made him a target. He and his family fled to Scandinavia. Finally, in 1941 he traveled to Los Angeles, where he continued to write and collaborate with other German writers in exile there. Most of his great plays were written between 1937 and 1941, including *Mother Courage and her Children*, and *The Life of Galileo*.

After the war Americans became terrified of the growth of Communism. In 1947 Brecht was called to appear before the House

Committee for Un-American Activities in order to investigate the "communist subversion" of Hollywood. Although he was not an official member of America's communist party, Brecht immediately left the United States for Switzerland, where he was reunited with Helen Wiegel. They travelled to East Berlin in 1948 and together thay set up the Berliner Ensemble with full support from the communist regime. Brecht died of a heart attack on August 14, 1956.

Brecht's Theatre

Brecht wanted to create theatre that was instructive but also entertaining, based on the simplest form of narrative, the story. His plays include elements from Chinese, Japanese, and Indian theatre, as well as Shakespeare and Greek tragedy, but he soon developed a unique style suited to his own vision. He insisted that spectators must be reminded that they are watching a play and did not want his plays to evoke the kind of emotional response that prevented the audience from thinking objectively and eventually taking social action. His theatrical innovations and his belief that the actor should not try to 'become' the character led to a new style of acting and directing.

He called his work with the Berliner Ensemble "epic theatre". Epic theatre uses an episodic plot structure, contains little cause and effect between scenes, and has cumulative character development. Other theatrical devices, including scene titles and projections, helped to achieve what Brecht called the 'Verfremsdung effeckt'. This has been translated as the 'Alienation Effect', but 'distancing' may be a more helpful expression. The aim is to promote critical detachment and objectivity in the audience, rather than emotion

SUMMARY OF THE PLOT

The Caucasian Chalk Circle was first produced in English in 1948. The prologue to the play is a dispute about land, and the story of the Chalk Circle is told as a kind of parable to solve the problem. Based on a Chinese legend, it tells the story of a struggle for possession of a child between its aristocratic mother, who deserts him during a revolution, and Grusha, the servant girl who takes responsibility for the child. The first half of the play recounts the adventures of Grusha, who flees into the mountains with the child of the Governor's Wife after the revolution. The second part of the play deals with the career of Adzak, the judge, a drunken corrupt figure. The Governor's Wife returns to claim Michael, the child she has abandoned, and Adzak has to decide who is the true parent. He applies the test of the Chalk Circle, and Grusha, who gives up her struggle for the child rather than harm him, is seen to be the true mother. Grusha and Simon are reunited. The story illustrates the Singer's point that 'what there is shall belong to those who are good for it'.

THE SCENE IN CONTEXT

The extract here comes from the beginning of the play after we see the Governor and his Wife going in procession to church with their soldiers and servants. In the scene, naturalistic moments, like the encounter between the Soldier and Grusha, are mixed with non-naturalistic elements. These include the Singer/Storyteller, the use of a Chorus and Brecht's suggestion that some characters, e.g. the Governor and his Wife, wear masks. The purpose of these devices is to help to 'distance' or 'de-familiarize' the emotional responses of the audience to the characters. For example, the Singer directs our attention to the significance of what is happening on stage and puts it in a wider context. His comments on Grusha's actions and motives prevent us from identifying too closely with her. For Brecht what matters is the story and the points he wants to make rather than presenting individual psychology. In spite of this, Simon and Grusha, in this extract, come across as real people, concerned about their own lives as much as the progress of the war.

The Caucasian Chalk Circle

By

Bertolt Brecht

CAST LIST

THE SINGER/STORYTELLER

THE SOLDIER (SIMON CHACHAVA)

GRUSHA

THE GOVERNOR

THE GOVERNOR'S WIFE

THE ADJUTANT

PALACE GUARDS

TWO DOCTORS

TWO ARCHITECTS

SERVANTS

Scene Two

Easter morning. Outside the Palace Gate. Mediaeval Georgia.

THE SINGER The city lies still.
    On the church square the pigeons preen themselves.
    A soldier of the palace guard
    Is jesting with the kitchen maid
    As she comes up from the river with a bundle.

A girl tries to pass through the gateway, a bundle of large green leaves under her arm.

THE SOLDIER What! The young lady is not in church? Shirking service?

GRUSHA I was all ready to go. But they wanted one more goose for the Easter banquet. And they asked me to fetch it. I know something about geese.

THE SOLDIER A goose? *(feigning suspicion)* I'd like to see that goose. **(Grusha** *doesn't understand)* One has to be on one's guard with women. They say: 'I only went to fetch a goose', and it turns out to be something quite different.

GRUSHA *Grusha walks resolutely toward him and shows him the goose* There it is. And if it isn't a fifteen pound goose, and they haven't stuffed it with corn, I'll eat the feathers.

THE SOLDIER A queen of a goose. It will be eaten by the Governor himself. So the young lady has been down to the river again?

GRUSHA Yes, at the poultry farm.

THE SOLDIER I see! At the poultry farm, down by the river. Not higher up, near those – those willows?

GRUSHA I go to the willows only to wash linen.

THE SOLDIER *insinuatingly* Exactly.

GRUSHA Exactly what?

THE SOLDIER *winking* Exactly that.

GRUSHA Why shouldn't I wash my linen near the willows?

THE SOLDIER *with exaggerated laughter* 'Why shouldn't I wash my linen near the willows'! That's a good one, that is!

GRUSHA I don't understand the soldier. What's so good about it?

THE SOLDIER *slyly* If someone knew what someone's told, she'd grow hot, she'd grow cold.

Grusha I don't know what I could know about those willows.

The Soldier Not even if there were a bush opposite? From which everything could be seen? Everything that happens there when a certain person is washing linen?

Grusha What happens there? Won't the soldier say what he means and have done with it?

The Soldier Something happens. And perhaps something can be seen.

Grusha Could the soldier mean that – once in a while on a hot day – I put my toes in the water? For otherwise there's nothing.

The Soldier And more – the toes and more.

Grusha More what? At most the foot.

The Soldier The foot and a little bit more. *(he laughs heartily)*

Grusha Simon Chachava, you ought to be ashamed of yourself! To sit in a bush on a hot day and wait till someone comes along and puts her leg in the river! And most likely with another soldier! *(she runs off)*

The Soldier *shouting after her* Not with another soldier! *(he runs off after her)*

The Singer The city lies still, but why are there armed men?
The Governor's palace lies at peace
But why is it a fortress?

70

*(From the doorway at the left a fat prince enters quickly. He stands still and looks around. Before the gateway at the right two Ironshirts are waiting. Noticing them, the prince walks quickly past them, signs to them, then exits quickly. One Ironshirt exits through the gateway, the other remains on guard. Muffled voices come from different sides in the rear: 'To your posts!' The palace is surrounded. Distant church bells. Enter through the doorway the procession and the **Governor**'s family returning from church.)*

Then the Governor returned to his palace
Then the fortress was a trap
Then the goose was plucked and roasted

Then the goose was no longer eaten
Then noon was no longer the hour to eat
Then noon was the hour to die.

GOVERNOR'S WIFE *in passing* It's quite impossible to live in this slum. But Georgi, of course, builds only for his little Michael. Never for me. Michael is everything, everything for Michael.

GOVERNOR Did you hear Brother Kazbeki bid me a 'Happy Easter'? That's all very well, but as far as I know it didn't rain in Nukha last night. It rained where Brother Kazbeki was. Where was Brother Kazbeki?

ADJUTANT That will have to be investigated.

The procession turns into the gateway. A rider walks towards the **Governor***.*

ADJUTANT Don't you want to listen to the rider from the capital, Your Excellency? He arrived this morning with confidential papers.

GOVERNOR *in passing* Not before the banquet, Shalva!

ADJUTANT *to the rider, while the procession disappears into the palace* The Governor doesn't wish to be disturbed by military reports before the banquet. The afternoon His Excellency will devote to conferences with prominent architects who have also been invited to the banquet. Here they are already.

(Enter three men. As the rider goes off, the **Adjutant** *greets the* **Architects***)*

Gentlemen, His Excellency is awaiting you at the banquet. His entire time will be devoted to you. To the great new plans. Come, let us go!

ARCHITECT 1 We are impressed that His Excellency thinks of building in spite of the disquieting rumours that the war in Persia has taken a turn for the worst.

ADJUTANT All the more reason for building! That's nothing. Persia is far away. The garrison here would let itself be chopped into pieces for its Governor.

*(Uproar from the palace. Shrill screams of a woman. Orders are shouted. Dumbfounded, the **Adjutant** moves towards the gateway. An Ironshirt steps out and holds him up at the point of a lance.)*

What's going on here? Put down that lance, you dog!

(to the palace guard, furiously)

Disarm him! Can't you see an attempt is being made on the Governor's life?

*The palace guard Ironshirts refuse to obey. Staring coldly, indifferently, at the **Adjutant**, they watch the proceedings without interest. The **Adjutant** fights his way into the palace.*

ARCHITECT 2 The Princes! Don't you realise that the Princes met last night in the capital? And that they are against the grand Duke and his governors? Gentlemen, we'd better make ourselves scarce.

They rush off.

THE SINGER Oh, the blindness of the great! They walk like gods   70
Great over bent backs, sure
Of hired fists, trusting
In their power which has already lasted so long.
But long is not forever.
Oh, wheel of Fortune! Hope of the people!

*(from the gateway, enter the **Governor** with a grey face, manacled, between two soldiers armed to the teeth)*

Walk, Your Highness, walk even now with head up.
From your palace the eyes of many foes follow you!
You no longer need an architect, a carpenter will do.
    You will not move into a new palace, but into a little hole in the ground.
Just look about you once more, you blind man!
Does all you once possessed still please you?
Between the Easter mass and the banquet
    You are walking to the place from which no one returns.
When the houses of the great collapse
Many little people are slain.

Those who had no share in the fortunes of the mighty
Often have a share in their misfortunes. The plunging wain
Drags the sweating beasts with it into the abyss.

(**Servants** come rushing through the gateway in panic)

SERVANTS in confusion
The hampers! –
Take them all into the third courtyard! Food for five days! –
Her Ladyship has fainted! Someone must carry her down. She
must get away. –
And what about us? We'll be slaughtered like chickens. It's the
old story. – Jesus and Mary, what's going to happen? There's
already bloodshed in the town, they say. –
Nonsense, the Governor has just been asked politely to appear at
a Princes' meeting.
Everything will be all right. I have this on the best authority.

Two **doctors** rush into the courtyard.

FIRST DOCTOR trying to restrain the other Niko Mikadze, it is your
duty as a doctor to attend Natella Abashvili.

SECOND DOCTOR My duty? It's yours!

FIRST DOCTOR Niko Mikadze, who is in charge of the child today?
You or me?

SECOND DOCTOR Do you really think Mihka Loladze, I'm going to
stay another minute in this cursed house for that little brat?

(They start fighting. All one hears is: 'You neglect your duty!' and 'Duty
be damned!' Then the **second doctor** knocks down the first.)

SECOND DOCTOR Oh, go to hell! (**Doctors** exit)

SERVANTS There's time enough before night. The soldiers won't be
drunk till then.
Does anyone know if they've started a mutiny yet? –
The Palace Guard has ridden away. –
Doesn't anyone know what's happened?

GRUSHA Meliva the fisherman says a comet with a red tail has been seen in the sky over the capital. That means bad luck.

SERVANTS Yesterday they were saying in the capital that the Persian War is lost. – The Princes have started a great revolt.
There's a rumour that the Grand Duke has already fled.
All his Governors are to be hanged. – The likes of us will be left alone.
I have a brother in the Ironshirts.

Enter the soldier **Simon Chachava**, *searching the crowd for* **Grusha**.

THE ADJUTANT *appearing in the doorway*
Everyone into the third courtyard. All hands help with the packing!

He drives the servants out. **Simon** *finally finds* **Grusha**.

SIMON There you are at last, Grusha! What are you going to do?

GRUSHA Nothing. If the worst comes to the worst, I've a brother with a farm in the mountains. But what about you?

SIMON Don't worry about me. *(polite again)* Grusha Vachnadze, your desire to know my plans fills me with satisfaction. I've been ordered to accompany Madam Natella Abashvili as her guard.

GRUSHA But hasn't the Palace Guard mutinied?

SIMON *serious* That's a fact.

GRUSHA But isn't it dangerous to accompany the woman?

SIMON In Tiflis they say: Isn't stabbing dangerous for the knife?

GRUSHA You're not a knife. You're a man, Simon Chachava. What has this woman to do with you?

SIMON The woman has nothing to do with me. But I have my orders and so I go.

GRUSHA The soldier is a pig-headed man; he gets himself into danger for nothing – nothing at all. *(as she is called from the palace)*

Now I must go into the third courtyard. I'm in a hurry.

SIMON As there's a hurry we oughtn't to quarrel. For a good quarrel one needs time. May I ask if the young lady still has parents?

GRUSHA No, only a brother.

SIMON As time is short – the second question would be: Is the young lady as healthy as a fish in water?

GRUSHA Perhaps once in a while a pain in the right shoulder; but otherwise strong enough for any work. So far no one has complained.

SIMON Everyone knows that. Even if it's Easter Sunday and there's the question who shall fetch the goose, then it's she. The third question is this: Is the young lady impatient? Does she want cherries in winter?

GRUSHA Impatient, no. But if a man goes to war without any reason, and no message comes, that's bad.

SIMON A message will come. *(**Grusha** is again called from the palace)* And finally the main question…

GRUSHA Simon Chachava, because I've got to go to the third courtyard and I'm in a hurry, the answer is 'Yes'.

SIMON *very embarrassed* Hurry, they say, is the wind that blows down the scaffolding. But they also say: The rich don't know what hurry is. I come from…

GRUSHA Kutsk.

SIMON So the young lady has already made enquiries? Am healthy, have no dependents, earn ten piastres a month, as a paymaster twenty, and am asking honorably for your hand.

GRUSHA Simon Chachava, that suits me.

SIMON *taking from his neck a thin chain from which hangs a little cross* This cross belonged to my mother, Grusha Vachnadze. The chain is silver. Please wear it.

GRUSHA I thank you, Simon. *(he fastens it around her neck)*

Simon Now I must harness the horses. The young lady will understand that. It would be better for the young lady to go into the third courtyard. Otherwise there'll be trouble.

Grusha Yes, Simon. *(they stand together undecided)*

Simon I'll just take the woman to the troops who've remained loyal. When the war's over, I'll come back. In two weeks. Or three. I hope my intended won't get tired waiting for my return.

Grusha Simon Chachava, I shall wait for you.
Go calmly into battle, soldier.
The bloody battle, the bitter battle
From which not everyone returns.
When you return I will be there.
I will be waiting for you under the green elm
I will be waiting for you under the bare elm
I will wait until the last soldier has returned
And even longer.
When you return from the battle
No boots will lie before the door
The pillow beside mine will be empty
My mouth will be unkissed.
When you return, when you return
You will be able to say: all is as it was.

Simon I thank you, Grusha Vachnadze, and farewell.

He bows low before her; she bows low before him. Then she runs off without looking round.

Staging the Scene

In Brecht's theatre, the director, designer, and composer had equal authority. This scene offers many opportunities for developing your skills in stage craft, and will provide useful preparation for performance support options at GCSE. The stage designer had a special function. As well as designing the sets and costumes, the designer was expected to produce a series of sketches of key moments in the action. These were used during rehearsals, to help the actors focus on the significant elements in the play. Brecht made the following comments about the setting of *The Caucasian Chalk Circle*:

> *The play's setting needs to be very simple. The varying backgrounds can be indicated by some form of projection; at the same time the projections must be artistically valid. What is going on onstage is not supposed to be a slice of some larger occurrence, just the part of it to be seen at this precise spot outside the palace gate. (Nor is the size of the palace to be conveyed in spatial terms).*

SET DESIGN

Although Brecht suggests that the design should be simple, the set for this scene is likely to be challenging, as a large number of actors are involved and a number of different events take place.

- Read the extract carefully. Examine your performance space, and consider your resources.

- Make a number of different sketches for the set. How will you indicate the Palace Gate – screens, projections, two posts and a crossbeam?

- How might you use different stage levels to heighten the effect of the scene?

- Identify three to four 'key moments' from the scene.

- Make a sketch of each moment, indicating the position of the actors in each one. How will you arrange them so as to achieve the maximum dramatic effect?

- Place the actors in freeze frames, according to your sketches. If you are not happy with the result, alter your sketches accordingly.

MUSIC AND SOUND EFFECTS

Music and songs were key elements in many of Brecht's plays. The score for *The Caucasian Chalk Circle* was designed not to evoke atmosphere but to support the text and often comment on it. Find some music that you think will add to your performance of the extract. Your choice will help to determine the style of your presentation. For example, you'll achieve different effects by the use of mediaeval music or folk songs.

- Look through the extract and find moments where sound effects could heighten the dramatic effect.

- Decide what sounds or music might accompany the flirtatious moments between Simon and Grusha.

- Find or create a series of sound effects that suggest the violent upheavals inside the Palace.

- How will your choice of music and sound effects show the contrast between the quiet passages and the chaos and upheaval of the revolution?

- How will you make sure that the use of music and sound effects will not interfere with the action, and in particular with the words of the Singer?

- Make a sound tape of all the effects you have chosen

COSTUMES AND MASKS

The play's setting is medieval Georgia, but you have considerable freedom to select the time frame and location you want to suggest – it might be mediaeval, or even modern. The colours and trimmings of the various garments you use can help to suggest the time and setting of the play.

A simple tunic, leggings and boots will be sufficient for the soldiers. Their weapons could be lances and swords. The Adjutant's rank could be indicated by the addition of a sash. If you have access to modern uniforms, you may decide to use them, while still using 'medieval' costumes for the other characters. For the servants you'll need long dark skirts and trousers, shawls and loose jackets.

The Governor and his Wife might wear cloaks in elaborate designs and strong colours. Brecht suggests that they should wear masks. Compared to the simple humanity of Simon and Grusha, they hardly appear to be real characters.

■ Run the scene, using masks for all the characters except Simon and Grusha.

■ How does it alter the effect of the scene? What does it feel like to act with characters who are not wearing masks?

■ Research the different kinds of theatrical masks, using a library and the Internet.

Lavish costumes and half-face masks in the RSC production directed by William Gaskill in 1962.

Exploring the Scene

Aims

The following activities will help you to:

English Framework Objective	Activity
(S&L12) Use a range of drama techniques to explore issues, ideas and meanings	B, D, E F, G
(R2) Synthesise information from a range of sources	H
(R14) Analyse the language, form and dramatic impact of the scene	A, C
(R12) Analyse and discuss the use of rhetorical devices in the text	G
(W12) Exploit the potential of presentational devices	F
(S&L10) Contribute to the organisation of group activity	B, C, D, G
(S&L5) Compare different points of view, identifying and evaluating differences and similarities	G
(R7) Compare the presentation of ideas, values or emotions in related or contrasting texts	H

EXPLORING CHARACTERS

A. Simon and Grusha

Taking on the character of Simon or Grusha will present actors with special challenges. We see the larger events of the play reflected in the reactions of these two ordinary people and the audience needs to find them sympathetic if the scene is to be effective. Their language is formal but their behaviour is naturalistic.

1. Read the scene carefully.
2. Make a list for Simon, including all the facts you learn about him from the scene.
3. Make another list for Grusha, including the facts you learn about her.
4. Identify three or four key characteristics about each of them – e.g. Simon's habit of quoting folk sayings.
5. At what point in the scene do we learn that they already know each other's names?
6. How does this change our view of them?
7. Make a list of Simon's priorities for a wife.
8. What is he able to offer Grusha?
9. What do you think her priorities for a husband might be?

B. Exploring Character – Distance or Alienation

Brecht suggests three ways of helping actors to achieve a kind of 'distance' from the characters they are portraying:

(a) Changing the speech into the third person – to allow the actor the right attitude of detachment
(b) Changing it into the past – to give the speaker a sense of perspective
(c) Speaking the stage directions out loud – to provide a clash between two tones of voice.

In groups
The following activities will help you to understand the effect of these changes.

1. Choose a section from the extract and try saying your lines in the third person – He said/she said….e.g.:

    GRUSHA Grusha says she is all ready to go. But they want one more goose for the Easter banquet. And they asked her to fetch it. Grusha knows something about geese.

2. Now change your lines into the past tense – e.g.

    GRUSHA I didn't understand the soldier. What was so good about it?

3. Now say your lines and also include the stage directions, but in a different tone of voice – e.g:

> **GRUSHA** Grusha walks resolutely toward him and shows him the goose. There it is. And if it isn't a fifteen pound goose, and they haven't stuffed it with corn, I'll eat the feathers.

4. Much of the dialogue between Simon and Grusha is already written in the third person. Choose a section from the second scene where Simon proposes to Grusha. Change the lines into the first person – e.g:

> **GRUSHA** You are a pig-headed man; you get yourself into danger for nothing – nothing at all. (*as she is called from the palace*) Now I must go into the third courtyard. I'm in a hurry.
>
> **SIMON** As there's a hurry we oughtn't to quarrel. For a good quarrel one needs time. May I ask if you still have parents?

How do these changes alter the relationship between Simon and Grusha and the effect of the scene?

EXPLORING ALTERNATIVES

C. Editing and Adapting the Play

Apart from beggars, soldiers, servants and wedding guests, there are more than 50 characters in the play. But as Brecht pointed out, 'The bit players can in some cases play several parts at once'. He also said that 'One good actor is worth a whole battalion of extras'.

In groups

1. Work in a small group. Decide how many extras might be available to take part in a performance of the extract.

2. How will you allocate the various parts? Which characters are the least significant?

3. If you have a number of extras, organize those playing the servants so that each one has some lines of dialogue.

4. What cuts will you need to make to the script if you decide to leave out some characters?

5. What changes would you make to the script if you had only two actors available?

cont...

> **6.** What other ways can you find to convey the information in the Singer's lines – for example by pre-recording them?
>
> **7.** How will you convey the news of the attack on the Palace and the capture of the Governor – by using an overhead projector, tape recording, placards?

D. Choral Speaking

Work in groups of 3 or 4.

55, 57, 59

1. Re-arrange the Singer's lines, dividing them among several voices, so that you achieve the effect of a chorus.

2. Listen carefully to the result and try to find contrasting voices among the people in your group.

3. Explore how variations of **pace** and **rhythm** may help to communicate the meaning of the text.

4. Experiment with placing the speakers in different positions or on different **levels**.

5. Observe the variations you can achieve by asking the speakers to stand still or having them move around as they speak.

6. Take it in turns to stand outside the group and evaluate how effectively the narration is conveyed.

7. Present the result to the rest of the class and discuss how different effects were achieved and the meaning communicated.

E. Marking the Moment

The purpose of this strategy is to select significant moments that help to provide insight into the characters' feelings and motives. Identify a number of these moments in the scene. As you play the scene, you can mark them in a variety of ways. For example, you might:

- freeze the action in a still image
- use captions or placards that provide a title for the moment
- ask the characters to speak their thoughts aloud
- use lighting to emphasise the moment.

F. Writing

1. Find an account of an incident in history or an event in a newspaper.
2. Divide it into a series of episodes.
3. Give each episode in the story a different title.
4. Write a short scene for each episode.
5. Create a series of placards to illustrate the stages of development of the story.
6. Present your scenes to the rest of the group.
7. How does this treatment change the way we feel about the story?

G. Media

Notice how Brecht suggests the offstage events through the rumours shared by the characters. The violent occurrences are kept at a distance but we see their effects in the behaviour and dialogue of the soldiers and servants.

 Presentation

In groups

1. Work in a small group. Read the extract aloud, paying particular attention to the dialogue among the servants. Make a list of every fact and supposition that is mentioned, e.g. the news that the Palace Guard has mutinied.
2. Work with a small group to prepare a news report for radio or television, detailing everything that is known about the revolution in the city, the reaction of the prince and the fate of the Governor.
3. Include interviews between a news reporter standing at the Palace Gate and the soldiers and servants.
4. Deliver the news report, or record it on audiotape or videotape.
5. Evaluate the effectiveness of your work and that of the other groups. Which group has succeeded in incorporating all the facts or rumours supplied in the scene and interpreting them?

COMPARING TEXTS – STYLE

Brecht developed a very different style of dramatic presentation and since the work of the Berliner Ensemble many directors and playwrights have worked in this style. Joan Littlewood, who first directed *A Taste of Honey* was a great advocate of the Brechtian style of dramatic presentation. There are many plays written for production in the Brechtian style, *A Memory of Lizzie* in the play collection *Sepia and Song* by Foxton is a good example.

H. Brechtian style

1. Compare *The Caucasian Chalk Circle* to *Hobson's Choice*. In what ways do the styles of the plays differ?
2. What typically Brechtian dramatic techniques can you find in *The Caucasian Chalk Circle*?
3. Can you find any of these techniques in *A Taste of Honey*?
4. How does the style of *A Taste of Honey* differ to that of *Billy Liar*?
5. Compare the style of *A Memory of Lizzie* to that of *The Caucasian Chalk Circle*.

A Taste of Honey
Shelagh Delaney

SHELAGH DELANEY

Shelagh Delaney was born in Salford, near Manchester, in 1939. She left school at 16 and took a number of jobs including shop assistant and cinema usherette. She was always interested in writing, and it was while working on a novel that she saw a play by Terence Rattigan, *Variations on a Theme*. In a strange parallel with Harold Brighouse, also born in Salford, she took exception to the polite drawing-room manners of this sophisticated comedy and decided that she could do better herself.

Delaney wanted to see the lives of ordinary people depicted on stage, particularly those who are disadvantaged by lack of money or social status. Theatrical portrayals of working-class people had often been restricted to comic or servant characters. However in the late 1950s a group of young dramatists, including such authors as Harold Pinter, Arnold Wesker and John Osborne saw working-class characters, environments and issues as important subjects for the stage. It was in this atmosphere of increased interest in social realism that the teenage Shelagh Delaney, writing from direct experience of working-class life in the industrial north of England, decided to turn her novel into the play that became *A Taste of Honey*.

The play challenged contemporary expectations of suitable subject matter in its portrayal of relatively unexplored issues such as mixed race relationships, homosexuality and single parenthood. At that time, Joan Littlewood, artistic director of the Theatre Royal in Stratford East was challenging the Lord Chamberlain's Office, the government department which enforced censorship on the theatre. Because of this, Delaney chose to send her potentially controversial play to Littlewood.

Joan Littlewood was one of Britain's most innovative theatrical directors. She founded her company, Theatre Workshop, in the 1930s and toured socially significant plays to schools, factories and communities unused to conventional theatre going. The company acquired a permanent home in Stratford in East London, and here Littlewood continued to pioneer new directorial methods and promote new writing. As well as spending time investigating the characters and the background to a play, actors were required to improvise around situations in the script, and exchange parts with each other. Scripts, including *A Taste of Honey*, were often altered and developed in this way.

A *Taste of Honey* was an instant success when it opened in Stratford East in 1958 and was later transferred to a West End theatre. A successful film version was released in 1962, starring Rita Tushingham. Delaney's career, particularly as a scriptwriter for film and television, continued to flourish.

SUMMARY OF THE PLOT

When Shelagh Delaney's play *A Taste Of Honey* was premiered back in the fifties, it was considered shocking. Not only did it portray a single mother pregnant with a black sailor's child, it featured a gay young man who befriends her. Nowadays, the shock factor is minimal, but the play is still a powerful picture of a dysfunctional family, and it helped to start the trend for a new realism and honesty in the theatre.

The central theme of the play is the relationship between the mother and daughter, Helen and Jo. Helen, Jo's forty-year-old mother, goes off to marry her new boyfriend Peter, leaving her teenage daughter to spend Christmas alone in their dismal rented flat. While she is away, Jo has a brief affair with a Nigerian sailor, who later returns to his ship. She becomes pregnant. Geof, a gay art student, moves in with her, sleeps on her couch and takes care of her. Helen returns when Peter leaves her for another woman. When she discovers the situation she decides to take care of Jo herself and after getting rid of Geof, she goes out for a drink. The play ends with Jo alone in the flat, singing a nursery rhyme, unaware that Geof has gone.

THE SCENE IN CONTEXT

In this scene we meet Helen as she is preparing to leave for her wedding with her boyfriend Peter. Jo, who has a heavy cold and has not been invited, does not share her excitement. We see the tense relationship between Helen and Jo, who wants to leave school, get a job and escape from her mother.

A Taste of Honey

By

Shelagh Delaney

CAST LIST

HELEN, a forty-year old woman

JO, her seventeen-year old daughter

ACT ONE

Scene Two

Setting: A comfortless flat in Salford, Lancashire, 1958.

*(Music. Wedding bells. **Helen** dances on with an assortment of fancy boxes, containing her wedding clothes.)*

HELEN Jo! Jo! Come on. Be sharp now. (*Jo comes on in her pyjamas. She has a heavy cold*) For God's sake give me a hand. I'll never be ready. What time is it? Have a look at the church clock.

JO A quarter past eleven, and the sun's coming out.

HELEN Oh! Well, happy the bride the sun shines on.

JO Yeah, and happy the corpse the rain rains on. You're not getting married in a church, are you?

HELEN Why, are you coming to throw bricks at us? Of course not. Do I look all right? Pass me my fur. Oh! My fur! Do you like it?

JO I bet someone's missing their cat.

HELEN It's a wedding present from that young man of mine. He spends his money like water, you know, penny wise, pound foolish. Oh! I am excited. I feel twenty-one all over again. Oh! You would have to catch a cold on my wedding day. I was going to ask you to be my bridesmaid too.

JO Don't talk daft.

HELEN Where did you put my shoes? Did you clean 'em? Oh! They're on my feet. Don't stand there sniffing, Jo. Use a handkerchief.

JO I haven't got one.

HELEN Use this, then. What's the matter with you? What are you trying to hide?

JO Nothing.

HELEN Don't try to kid me. What is it? Come on, let's see.

JO It's nothing. Let go of me. You're hurting.

HELEN What's this?

JO A ring.

HELEN I can see it's a ring. Who gave it to you?

JO A friend of mine.

HELEN Who? Come on. Tell me. (**Helen** *breaks the cord and gets the ring*) You should have sewn some buttons on your pyjamas if you didn't want me to see. Who gave it to you?

JO My boy friend. He asked me to marry him.

HELEN Well, you silly little bitch. You mean the lad you've been knocking about with while we've been away?

JO Yes.

HELEN I could choke you.

JO You've already had a damn good try.

HELEN You haven't known him five minutes. Has he really asked you to marry him?

Jo Yes.

HELEN Well, thank God for the divorce courts! I suppose just because I'm getting married you think you should.

Jo Have you got the monopoly?

HELEN You stupid little devil! What sort of a wife do you think you'd make? You're useless. It takes you all your time to look after yourself. I suppose you think you're in love. Anybody can fall in love, do you know that? But what do you know about the rest of it?

Jo Ask yourself.

HELEN You know where that ring should be? In the ashcan with everything else. Oh! I could kill her, I could really.

Jo You don't half knock me about. I hope you suffer for it.

HELEN I've done my share of suffering if I never do any more. Oh, Jo, you're only a kid. Why don't you learn from my mistakes? It takes half your life to learn from your own.

Jo You leave me alone. Can I have my ring back, please?

HELEN What a thing to happen just when I'm going to enjoy myself for a change.

Jo Nobody's stopping you.

HELEN Yes, and as soon as my back's turned you'll be off with this sailor boy and ruin yourself for good.

Jo I'm already ruined.

HELEN Yes, it's just the sort of thing you'd do. You make me sick.

Jo You've no need to worry, Helen. He's gone away. He may be back in six months, but there again, he may…

HELEN Look, you're only young. Enjoy your life. Don't get trapped. Marriage can be hell for a kid.

Jo Can I have your hanky back?

Helen Where did you put it?

Jo This is your fault too.

Helen Everything's my fault. Show me your tongue.

Jo Breathing your 'flu bugs all over me.

Helen Yes, and your neck's red where I pulled that string.

Jo Will you get me a drink of water, Helen?

Helen No, have a dose of this. *(offering whisky)* It'll do you more good. I might just as well have one myself while I'm at it, mightn't I?

Jo You've emptied more bottles down your throat in the last few weeks that I would have thought possible. If you don't watch it, you'll end up an old down-and-out boozer knocking back the meths.

Helen It'll never come to that. The devil looks after his own, they say.

Jo He certainly takes good care of you. You look marvellous, considering.

Helen Considering what?

Jo The wear and tear on your soul.

Helen Oh well, that'll have increased its market value, won't it?

Jo Old Nick'll get you in the end.

Helen Thank God for that! Heaven must be a hell of a place. Nothing but repentant sinners up there, isn't it? All the pimps, prostitutes and politicians in creation trying to cash in on eternity and their little tin god. Where's my hat?

Jo Where's your husband?

Helen Probably drunk with his pals somewhere. He was going down to the house this morning to let some air in. Have you seen a picture of the house? Yes, you have. Do you like it? *(she peers and primps into the mirror)*

Jo Will you tell me something before you go?

Helen Oh! You can read all about that in books.

Jo What was my father like? *(**Helen** turns away)*

Helen Who?

Jo You heard! My father! What was he like?

Helen Oh! Him.

Jo Well, was he so horrible that you can't even tell me about him?

Helen He wasn't horrible. He was just a bit stupid, you know. Not very bright.

Jo Be serious, Helen.

Helen I am serious.

Jo Are you trying to tell me he was an idiot?

Helen He wasn't an idiot, he was just a bit – retarded.

Jo You liar!

Helen All right, I'm a liar.

Jo Look at me.

Helen Well, am I?

Jo No.

Helen Well, now you know.

Jo How could you give me a father like that?

Helen I didn't do it on purpose. How was I to know you'd materialize out of a little love affair that lasted five minutes?

Jo You never think. That's your trouble.

Helen I know.

Jo Was he like a…a real idiot?

Helen I've told you once. He was nice though, you know, a nice little feller!

Jo Where is he now, locked up?

Helen No, he's dead.

Jo Why?

Helen Why? Well, I mean. Death's something that comes to us all, and when it does come you haven't usually got time to ask why.

Jo It's hereditary, isn't it?

Helen What?

Jo Madness.

Helen Sometimes.

Jo Am I mad?

Helen Decide for yourself. Oh, Jo, don't be silly. Of course you're not daft. Not more so than anybody else?

Jo Why did you have to tell me that story? Couldn't you have made something up?

Helen You asked for the truth and you got it for once. Now be satisfied.

Jo How could you go with a half-wit?

Helen He had strange eyes. You've got 'em. Everybody used to laugh at him. Go on, I'll tell you some other time.

Jo Tell me now!

Helen Mind my scent!

Jo Please tell me. I want to understand.

Helen Do you think I understand? For one night, actually it was the afternoon, I loved him. It was the first time I'd ever really been with a man…

Jo You were married.

Helen I was married to a Puritan – do you know what I mean?

Jo I think so.

Helen And when I met your father I was as pure and unsullied as I fondly, and perhaps mistakenly, imagine you to be. It was the first time and though you can enjoy the second, third, even the fourth time, there's no time like the first, it's always there. I'm off now. I've got to go and find my husband. Now don't sit here sulking all day.

Jo I was thinking.

Helen Well, don't think. It doesn't do you any good. I'll see you when the honeymoon's over. Come on, give us a kiss. You may as well. It's a long time since you kissed me.

Jo Keep it for him.

Helen I don't suppose you're sorry to see me go.

Jo I'm not sorry and I'm not glad.

Helen You don't know what you do want.

Jo Yes, I do. I've always known what I want.

Helen And when it comes your way will you recognize it?

Jo Good luck, Helen.

Helen I'll be seeing you. Hey! If he doesn't show up I'll be back.

Jo Good luck, Helen.

*Exit **Helen**.*

Staging the Scene

SET DESIGN

A Taste of Honey was written as a naturalistic drama, but during its first production in Theatre Royal, Stratford, in 1958, the director, Joan Littlewood, placed a live orchestra on stage throughout the play. As you will see from the illustration, the set is impressionistic, rather than a realistic representation of a basement room.

- What particular features have been emphasised by the designer?
- Can you find reasons for these decisions?
- If you decide to perform the scene, how will you use lighting effectively?
- What kind of furniture and props will help to convey the atmosphere of the 'dingy basement room'?

A Taste of Honey, *Theatre Royal, Stratford.*

COSTUMES AND PROPS

Jo is wearing her pyjamas, and perhaps a dressing gown. Helen is on her way to her wedding, and has made some effort to look smart. During the scene she gets ready to go out, adding a fur stole or jacket, and perhaps a hat.

Research the clothes of the late 1950s, remembering that Helen is always short of money, but manages to look attractive in spite of this. You'll need a ring on a cord for Jo, and a handkerchief and whisky flask or bottle for Helen. Research too the hairstyles, furniture and houses of the period.

 ## MUSIC AND SOUND EFFECTS

Remembering that the director of the first production of the play chose to accompany the scenes with music, how could you use music to emphasise the mood of the scene? Would sound effects help to create the feeling of being in a city?

Exploring the Scene

Aims

The following activities will help you to:

English Framework Objective	Activity
(S&L12) Use a range of drama techniques to explore issues, ideas and meanings	B, D, E F, G, H
(S&L3) Develop interview techniques	F
(S&L8) Discuss and evaluate conflicting evidence	A, C, F I, J
(S&L14) Convey action and character in improvisation and performance	B, D, E F, G, H
(W9) Integrate diverse information into a coherent account	F

EXPLORING CHARACTERS

A. Jo and Helen

1. Write two lists of adjectives that describe Jo and Helen.

2. They seem to share a rather bitter sense of humour. Find examples of this in the scene.

3. Was Helen right to tell Jo the truth about her father?

4. Jo claims that she has always known what she wants. What do you think that this might be?

B. Thinking Aloud

In groups

1. Read the scene carefully. Pick out two or three **key moments** in the text where the thoughts and feelings of the characters are not entirely obvious.

2. Cast two of the group as Helen and Jo and listen as they read aloud or act out the scene. When they reach these moments, freeze the action and dialogue.

3. Using the technique of **thought-tracking**, ask other members of the group to reveal what each character is thinking at that moment, by speaking the character's thoughts aloud.

4. Continue with the scene until the next key moment is reached. Ask another two members of the group to speak the characters' thoughts aloud. Continue until each key moment you have identified has been explored.

C. Discussion

- Based on your reading of the scene, pick out examples of Helen's behaviour that tell us she is far from being a perfect mother.
- Can you find anything to say in her favour?
- How far is Jo to blame for the way her mother treats her?
- What evidence can you find that there is some affection between Jo and her mother?

EXPLORING THE THEMES AND IDEAS

D. Improvisation

In pairs

1. *Organisation*: Work with a partner. One of you takes on the role of Helen. The other is her fiancé.

cont...

Situation: Helen has not told her fiancé that she has a teenage daughter. How does she break the news to him? How does she describe Jo? Does she try to make Jo sound pleasant, or does she imply that Jo will not expect to be part of their new household?

Opening Line: HELEN There's something you ought to know.

2. *Organisation*: Work with a partner. A takes on the role of Helen. B chooses to be either Peter, Helen's new boyfriend or a close friend.

Situation: Helen is revealing her real feelings about her daughter.

Opening Line: HELEN You don't know what she's really like…

Reversal: Working with the same partner, change roles. B takes on the role of Jo, and A is either her friend Geof or another close friend. The situation and opening line remain the same.

E. Forum Theatre

In Forum Theatre, an improvised scene is presented to the rest of the group. The observers, can step in at any point during the scene, to make suggestions about its direction, add a role, or take over an existing role.

In groups

Organisation: A small group takes on the responsibility for playing this scene. One person in the group takes on the role of Helen. The others are social workers.

Situation: One of Jo's teachers has noticed that she looks ill. She alerts the Social Services and one or more social workers are sent to interview Helen.

Opening Line: SOCIAL WORKER What exactly is the matter with your daughter?

The attitudes of Helen and the Social Workers to child care are likely to be very different. How can the Social Workers persuade Helen that she needs to take more responsibility for Jo?

Run the scene. At any point those watching can interrupt the scene to suggest changes in the dialogue or action, take over a role or join in the improvisation in an additional role.

F. The Courtroom

As a class

Imagine that Helen has been taken to court because of her neglect of Jo. Find out as much as you can about the way a court operates. Make sure that the correct language is used and that formal procedures are observed. If anyone breaks the rules and is found in contempt of court, then he or she can be removed from the court.

1. Set up your space to resemble a courtroom.

2. Choose several people to play the magistrates, Helen's lawyer and any other extra characters that may be needed, for example teachers, school friends, neighbours, reporters and court officials.

3. Ask the magistrates to weigh the evidence and come to a decision about Jo's future.

Remember that evidence can be used either to support the charge of neglect or to deny it. Will Jo give evidence against her mother? The court may ask Helen to speak in her own defence. Maybe the social worker's report will convince the magistrates that Helen should be given another chance.

■ What conditions might the court impose?

■ How would Helen and Jo feel about the result of the inquiry?

■ Would it be likely to bring them closer together?

■ Write an account of the court proceedings for a local newspaper, including all the details that emerge about Helen and her relationship with Jo.

G. Monologues

On your own

Take on the role of either Helen, Jo, or Geof. Imagine that several years have passed since the scene took place. Write a monologue as one of these characters, looking back on the events and reflecting on them. Will you try to justify your own attitudes and behaviour or will you blame other people for any of your failures? What new events in your life will you include?

Present your monologue in role to the rest of the class.

H

H. Symbols

Sometimes playwrights use **symbols** in their work. What might the ring which Jo wears round her neck symbolize? Look at the section at the end of *The Caucasian Chalk Circle* where Simon gives Grusha a cross and chain.

- What might Simon's gift symbolise for him and for Grusha?
- How do Jo's ring and Simon's cross and chain differ in what they represent?
- What might have been the feelings and motives of those who gave and received them?

In Pairs

1. Work with a partner. Imagine that one of you is Grusha and the other is Jo. Each one tells the other about the circumstances in which she was given either the cross and chain or the ring.

2. Alternatively, working with a partner, you each take on the role of either Simon or Jo's boyfriend, the sailor. Again, explain what happened when you gave the gift to Grusha or Jo.

In Threes

3. Working in threes, choose one of the above activities. As the improvisation proceeds the third person provides a commentary on the events that are being described. This '**narrator**' may have a particular attitude about what has happened.

I. Writing for the Theatre

Shelagh Delaney wrote to Joan Littlewood, the Director of Theatre Workshop, with a copy of her first play.

Dear Miss Littlewood

Along with this letter comes a play, the first I have written…

A fortnight ago I didn't know the theatre existed, but a young man, anxious to improve my mind, took me to the Opera House in Manchester, and I came away after the performance having suddenly realized that at last, after nineteen years of life, I had discovered something that meant more to me than myself...The following day I bought a packet of paper and borrowed an unbelievable typewriter which I still have great difficulty in using. I set to and produced this little epic – don't ask me why – I'm quite unqualified for anything like this. But at least I finished it and if, from among the markings and the typing errors and the spelling mistakes, you can gather a little sense from what I have written – or a little nonsense – I should be extremely grateful for your criticism – though I hate criticism of any kind.

I want to write for the theatre, but I know so very little about it. I know nothing, have nothing – except a willingness to learn – and intelligence.

> Yours sincerely,
> Shelagh Delaney

These are Joan Littlewood's first impressions of the play:

There wasn't much of a plot...If the author had reread her script, she certainly hadn't pruned it. It remained as it had been when it emerged from that unbelievable typewriter. Most of the scenes didn't develop, largely because the author's thoughts were written down higgledy-piggledy. Was it worth salvaging? It was far too long. One would have to take care not to lose its freshness.

In spite of her reservations, Joan Littlewood produced *A Taste of Honey*, after making a number of changes to the script. She was not alone in having some criticisms of the play.

A Report from The Arts Council's Drama Panel:

This is a good bad play. It seems to have been dashed off in pencil in a school exercise book by a youngster who knows practically nothing about the theatre and rather more about life than she can at present digest. ...Miss Delaney writes with the confidence of sheer ignorance.

A Review:

It has been alleged against Shelagh Delaney that she wrote down the first thing that came into her head. But this is her great achievement.

A Taste of Honey is a boozed, exaggerated, late-night anecdote of a play which slithers unsteadily between farce and tragedy. It is written as if it were a film script, with an adolescent contempt for logic or form or practicality upon a stage.

Alan Brien in The Spectator

---

1. What does Shelagh Delaney's letter reveal about her character and background?

2. Alan Brien, the critic in The Spectator, seems uncertain whether he likes the play or not. What do you think he means by a 'boozed, exaggerated, late-night anecdote of a play'?

3. Do you agree with either of the critics' judgments? Alan Brien notes that the play is like a film-script, and the play was later made into a successful film.

4. Find a copy of the film on video and notice the differences in the same scene from the film. Which is the most successful in conveying the relationship between mother and daughter?

5. Write a review of the film.

COMPARING TEXTS – SOCIETY AND CULTURE

J. Themes for Comparison: Family Relationships and Sexual Relationships

The play *Billy Liar* was first produced two years after *A Taste of Honey* in 1960 and is also set in the north of England. *Billy Liar* depicts a 19 year old boy living with his lower middle class parents and grandmother in a very conventional way. Billy Fisher feels trapped in this conventional environment and creates a fictional world which is at times more real to him than real life. He is a compulsive liar and at the start of the play he is engaged to two girls and in love with another.

Read Act 1 of *Billy Liar*.

1. Compare the relationship of Billy with his father Geoffrey to that of Jo with Helen.

2. Compare the relationship Jo has with the Boy with the relationship Billy has with Barbara. Which is more honest and real?

Exploring and Comparing the Four Extracts

<table>
<tr><td colspan="2" align="center">## Aims
These activities will help you to:</td></tr>
<tr><th>English Framework Objective</th><th>Activity</th></tr>
<tr><td>(R9) Compare the themes and styles of two or more writers from different times</td><td>A, B, M</td></tr>
<tr><td>(R7) Compare the presentation of ideas, values and emotions in related or contrasting texts.</td><td>A, B, D, M</td></tr>
<tr><td>(R10) Comment on interpretations of the same text or idea in different media</td><td>N</td></tr>
<tr><td>(R12) Analyse and discuss the use of dramatic devices in a text</td><td>M</td></tr>
<tr><td>(R15) Extend your understanding of literary heritage</td><td>M, N</td></tr>
<tr><td>(S&L10) Contribute to the organisation of group activity</td><td>C, D, F, L</td></tr>
<tr><td>(S&L15) Write critical evaluations of performances</td><td>N</td></tr>
</table>

CHARACTERS AND THEMES

A. Lonely-Hearts

In groups

1. *Organisation*: Work in a group with even numbers, perhaps six or eight people.

   Situation: On a sheet of paper, each person in the group writes a lonely-hearts advertisement for one or more of the characters in the scenes in this book. Research the different kinds of conventions that are used in advertisements of this kind.

For example, for Petrucio the advertisement might read:

> Unconventional M seeks wealthy F for marriage, looks unimportant, gsh essential.

The name of the character should not be included at this point, but could be written on the back of the advertisement.

Development: Share the advertisements. Try to arrange the ads in pairs. You might decide to pair up either the most or the least compatible seeming partners. Now reveal the name of the person referred to in each ad. Have any of them been matched with the correct character from their scene?

Extensions: Write or improvise a conversation between one of the couples.

Create a wedding announcement and a wedding invitation for each of the couples.

B. Courtship and Marriage

- What different ideas about courtship and marriage are revealed in these plays?
- How have ideas about courtship, marriage and the place of women changed since these plays were first written?
- Do you think these different writers accepted the existing attitudes of society at the time, or do you notice any moments in the scenes where they seemed to want to undermine these attitudes?
- Many marriages in Britain today end in divorce – how far do you think that unrealistic expectations are to blame?
- Compare Simon and Grusha's priorities and those of Maggie in the extract from *Hobson's Choice*.
- Which of the potential marriages in the extracts do you think is likely to prove the happiest?
- Which partners are least well suited to each other?
- Make a list of your own priorities for a life partner.
- Work with a partner. Take it in turn to interview each other about your list of priorities. Justify your choices.

C. Improvisation

In groups

1. *Organisation*: Work in a small group. Choose a couple from one of the scenes in this book.

   Situation: Each group creates a series of tableaux or **freeze frames** of wedding photographs. As well as the bride and groom, other members of the family may be included. How will you indicate the relative dominance of the bride or the groom in the relationship? Is it possible to suggest by stance and attitude the time period from which they come?

   Development: Share each tableau with the rest of the class. Is it possible to identify the scene from which the couple has come? Can you tell from these images whether the couple has a chance of happiness?

D. TV Talk Show

As a class

1. *Organisation*: Everyone chooses a role, either male or female, from one of the scenes in the book. Re-read the scene, and remind yourself of the personality and attitudes of the character you have chosen.

   Situation: The setting is a television studio. The teacher, and/or one member of the class adopts the role of TV host and introduces a discussion about marriage.

   Opening Line: TALK SHOW HOST Is there any such thing as a happy marriage?

   Whoever wishes to join in introduces him or herself – e.g. "My name is Simon Chachava. Speaking as a soldier –" (*The Caucasian Chalk Circle*) or "My name is Maggie Mossop. I believe that women should be equal partners in marriage" (*Hobson's Choice*). Each "guest" is likely to present a different attitude to the subject of marriage, and the criteria for a good partner in life.

   Development: The talk show host(s) sums up the attitudes to marriage that the various 'guests' have presented.

A MATCH MADE IN HEAVEN?

The following activities all take as their starting point two additional drama texts. In each case the text is a poem linked by the theme of marriage to the four extracts. Both the poems and the activities provide ideal material for devised drama work.

E. Rules

In pairs

- Read the following poem.

- Decide whether the speaker is male or female.

- What difference does a change of gender make to the effect of the poem?

- Work with a partner and present the poem with one person speaking the lines and the other trying to carry out all they demand in action.

- How will you show the climax of the poem?

- Share the results with the rest of the group.

My Rules
by Shel Silverstein

If you want to marry me, here's what you'll have to do:
You must learn how to make a perfect chicken-dumpling stew.
And you must sew my holey socks,
And soothe my troubled mind,
And develop the knack for scratching my back,
And keep my shoes spotlessly shined.
And while I rest you must rake up the leaves,
And when it is hailing and snowing
You must shovel the walk…and be still when I talk,
And – hey – where are you going?

F. If you want to marry me …

In pairs

1. *Organisation*: Work with a partner. Call yourselves A and B.

   Situation: A has proposed to B. B announces his or her list of demands, based on the poem, although other items can be included.

   Opening Line: **B** If you want to marry me, here's what you'll have to do:

   Extension: Make up your own set of rules for a happy marriage. These can be serious, or absurd or outrageous. Improvise a scene where you announce your rules to your intended partner.

G. Marriage Examinations

Imagine that the government has decided to try to avoid so many marriages ending in divorce by demanding that couples intending to marry should first pass an examination.

1. Create the first five questions on the examination paper.
2. Exchange your questions with a friend and try to answer the questions they have set.
3. How might these questions be different if they were set in other times or cultures?
4. Create a 'marriage exam' for one of the couples from the scenes in this book.
5. Write the answers you think they might give to the questions you set.

H. Wedding Postponed

- Read the following poem carefully.
- What kind of wedding has been planned?
- Who exactly do you think is speaking?
- Make a list of as many possible explanations for the wedding being postponed as you can think of.
- Share your list with a partner.

Wedding Postponed
by Carl Sandburg.

The arrangements are changed.
We were going to marry at six o'clock.
Now we shall not marry at all.

The bridegroom was all ready.
And the best man of the bridegroom was ready.
The bride fixed out in orchids and a long veil,
The bride and six bridesmaids were all ready.

Then the arrangements changed.
The date was changed not from six o'clock till later,
The date was changed to no time at all, to never.

Why the arrangements were changed is a long story.
Tell half of it and it is better than nothing at all.
Tell it with a hint and a whisper and it is told wrong.

We know why it was put off,
Why the arrangements shifted,
Why the organist was told to go,
Why the minister ready for the ring ceremony
Was told to drive away and be quick about it, please.
We know this in all its results and circumstances.

The disappointment of the best man,
The sorry look on the faces of the bridesmaids,
We, who chose them out of many, we could understand.

And we told then only what is told here:
The arrangements are changed, there will be no wedding,
We shall not marry at all, not today, not tomorrow, no time.

I. It is with regret ...

1. Write a letter from the bride to the groom, or vice versa, the night before the wedding.

2. Write a newspaper announcement of the cancellation of the wedding.

3. Write a paragraph about either the bride or the groom, outlining what lies ahead for them. Will they find happiness?

J. Ten Years Later

H

1. Decide on one of the explanations for the postponement of the wedding that were suggested earlier and write a scene between the bride and groom, set ten years after the planned wedding. You will need to decide on some key points:

    ■ Did the bride and groom get married later?
    ■ Have they met each other since the wedding was cancelled?
    ■ How do they feel about each other now?
    ■ Will they discuss the reasons the wedding was cancelled?
    ■ Is the atmosphere of your scene sad or happy?

2. Use the device of '**cross-cutting**' to enhance the effect of your scene. In this technique, the order of events is altered by 'cutting' backwards and forwards to different moments. As well as changing the order of your scene, you might insert lines or verses from the poem to give this effect.

K. Choral Reading

In groups

1. Re-read the poem carefully.

2. Divide up the verses so that the poem can be spoken by a number of people, perhaps representing at different moments the bride and groom, the wedding guests, the minister and so on. Be careful to consider the effects of the different voices in your group, and the pace at which they say their lines.

3. Arrange the readers so that they form a tableau, or **freeze frame**, to represent those involved in the wedding.

4. As the poem proceeds, the various characters might turn their backs, or leave the group, so that finally the bride and groom are the last to speak.

DEVISED PERFORMANCE

L. Putting it Together

Several GCSE drama syllabuses offer the opportunity to devise a performance as part of the examination process.

In groups

- Work in a group to put together a devised presentation. You might use some of the material presented in this section, for example the poems. You might also decide to include some of the activities suggested in previous sections, extracts from the scenes, your own improvisations or other material you have found that deals with similar themes.

- You could present your piece as a documentary on Marriage, using conventions borrowed from film and TV.

- The presentation might begin with the group taking turns to read out a sequence of lonely-hearts advertisements, either found in newspapers and magazines, or specially written.

- Alternatively, you might choose to begin with a list of factual information, such as statistics for marriage and divorce.

- Think about how sound effects or romantic music and songs about love could be used to link the different segments of your presentation.

- Experiment with various ways of exploring the ideas and issues in your chosen material. Try to communicate your ideas dramatically, using as many different drama techniques as are appropriate.

- When you are satisfied with the structure of your piece, write it out as a script and give everyone a copy. Make sure that everyone understands his or her contribution to the performance.

- How will you make sure that all those in your group have an opportunity to demonstrate their skills in acting, design or technical support?

- Rehearse your presentation and share it with an audience.

COMPARING DRAMATIC TECHNIQUES

M. Analysing Scripts

Look carefully at two or three of the scenes in the book. How does the playwright capture our attention? How does the playwright give us information about:

- Time of day
- Location of the scene
- Approximate age and status of the characters
- What has happened previously?

Notice some of the dramatic techniques used by the playwrights. Which scenes include:

- Direct address to the audience
- Narration
- Music and songs
- Information provided to the audience but not known to at least some of the characters
- Symbols?

All of these plays have appealed to many different audiences down the years and are still frequently performed. Pick out your favourite scene and favourite character. What reasons can you give for your choice? Why do you think these plays continue to interest and amuse us today?

REVIEWING THE SCENES

N. Play Reviews

The theatre director Herbert Beerbohm Tree wrote the following reply to a hopeful playwright who had written to him asking for his opinion.

My dear Sir,

I have read your play. Oh my dear Sir.

Yours faithfully –
Herbert Beerbohm Tree

■ How do you think the aspiring playwright might have reacted to this letter?

---

1. Find two or three theatre reviews printed in current newspapers. Note how the writer conveys the impact of the play, the themes it deals with, the design and staging and the performances. Compare these reviews with cinema and television reviews. What difference can you find?

2. Find videos of the film versions of *The Taming of the Shrew*, *Hobson's Choice*, and *A Taste of Honey*. Why do you think that filmmakers have chosen to make new versions of these plays? Choose one of the films and write a review

3. Re-read some of the theatre reviews included here and write a review of one of the scenes you have watched. Try to be as honest as you can. Try to be objective, and make your comments as constructive as possible so that they will be helpful to others in the group.

   Don't forget to include comments on the following:

   >   Plot
   >   Themes
   >   Characterisation
   >   Dialogue
   >   Dramatic techniques
   >   The style of the piece
   >   Social and cultural influences
   >   The staging of the scene

4. If you have written or performed in a scene, write a review of the presentation, again as honestly as possible. Include comments on your own contributions.

Guidance for GCSE Drama

The activities in this book will be very helpful in working towards GCSE Drama examinations.

ACTING/PERFORMANCE FROM A TEXT

EDEXCEL, AQA and WJEC offer an Acting option, as well as the requirement to perform using a text as part of the coursework. Many of the suggested activities in this book are designed to promote the ability to explore a variety of characters and issues in depth, as well as providing experience in responding to texts, presenting work to others and evaluating the results.

In order to achieve good marks in Acting and Performance, candidates in these examinations are expected to be able to:

- Use appropriate vocal and physical skills (AQA) (WJEC) (EDEXCEL)
- Work in role to create a character (WJEC)
- Perform a role with belief and confidence; create and sustain a role/character with creativity and originality (AQA) (EDEXCEL)
- Contribute to the performance through using a variety of theatrical media (WJEC)
- Present a character or role to an audience (WJEC)
- Communicate clearly to an audience (EDEXCEL)
- Respond to the script showing understanding of its dramatic possibilities, including exploring relationships and comparisons between texts, dramatic styles and different cultures (AQA)
- Work towards a performance and carry out the author's or devising group's intentions through the ability to interpret a specific theme (WJEC)
- Evaluate the effectiveness of their work and that of others in both the process of development and the performance (AQA) (WJEC)

IMPROVISATION/DEVISED PERFORMANCE

EDEXCEL, AQA and WJEC offer a Devised Performance option. A script may be used as a starting point (EDEXCEL) and may include both extracts from existing texts – plays, verse or prose – as well as original and improvised work (AQA) (WJEC). In addition, AQA offers an Improvisation option. Improvisation is defined as any non-scripted work in drama and requires the ability to respond creatively to ideas as well as accepting and building on the responses of others.

This book offers a variety of ideas for improvisation after each scene that will provide valuable experience in improvisation. Many of the suggested activities could be adapted for inclusion in a devised performance. In order to achieve good marks in these options, candidates are expected to be able to:

- Use appropriate vocal and physical skills (AQA) (WJEC)
- Accept, create and sustain a role or character appropriate to the theme and situation (AQA) (EDEXCEL)
- Explore ideas in an expressive, perceptive and personal way (EDEXCEL)
- Experiment creatively with different forms and approaches (EDEXCEL)
- Respond critically, creatively and sensitively to a range of drama activities (WJEC)
- Select appropriate forms and convey ideas coherently (WJEC)
- Contribute within a theme to the process of devising (WJEC)
- Interpret a specific theme through a variety of theatrical media (WJEC)
- Respond to stimuli/texts/themes showing understanding of their dramatic possibilities, including exploring relationships and comparisons between work from different periods and cultures (AQA)
- Shape and structure a variety of theatrical and technical media towards a final performance (WJEC)
- Develop a good rapport with other performers (AQA) (EDEXCEL)
- Perform with confidence and expression (EDEXCEL)
- Evaluate the effectiveness of their work and that of others in both the process of development and the performance (AQA)

PRACTICAL DESIGN OPTIONS

Several examination boards offer practical performance support options as part of the coursework assessment process as well as devised and scripted performance options. The OCR syllabus includes a paper requiring knowledge of the skills used by performers, directors and stage-managers, as well as designers of set, lighting, sound, costume and make-up, and AQA offers practical design components as coursework options.

SET DESIGN

The designer's task is to present the work of the director and the actors in the most effective way. The decisions you make about the use of the performance space will directly affect the success of the scene – the key is to keep your design simple but effective. Consider the possibilities of your performance area. Proscenium arches, arena theatre, thrust stages, theatre in the round and promenade performances all offer different challenges and different advantages, as do the use of several levels. The mode of presentation should be appropriate to the style of the scene. Remember that the audience must be able to see all of the action.

Read the scene carefully, make rough sketches of the staging possibilities and discuss your ideas with the director. It is important, particularly for examination purposes, to keep a working sketchbook to record your ideas. Include:

- Details of preliminary research into the period in which the play is set
- Illustrations and photographs of previous productions
- A ground plan of the acting area
- A model of the set or stage plans to scale.

Some examination boards may require you to include in your portfolio an evaluation of your contribution to the production and of the performance itself. You might also include a set design that indicates the kind of staging you would like to create if you had no limitations of time, resources and budget.

COSTUME

> Costume is a growth, an evolution, and a most important, perhaps the most important, sign of the manners, customs, and mode of life of each century.
>
> *Oscar Wilde*

Costumes will make a powerful contribution to the success of the scene. Well designed or chosen costumes can heighten the impact of a particular character, convey period and atmosphere, alter the time in which the play is set, and help the actors to communicate their characters to the audience. The clothes themselves may help the actors gain insight into the characters that they are playing. Some costumes may restrict movement, and suggest ways of walking and sitting that will assist the actors in their characterisation. For example, soldiers' uniforms and weapons will help actors acquire a military stance, and the elaborate costumes for *The Taming of the Shrew* will encourage more stately, formal ways of moving.

The decisions you take about the colour of the costumes will also add impact to your presentation and influence the audience's response to the characters. Make sure that the colours you choose work together, unless you are aiming for stark contrasts. In *The Caucasian Chalk Circle*, the simple shape and colour of Grusha's dress will convey her lowly status in contrast to the strong colours and patterns worn by the Governor and his Wife. Maggie's plain dress in *Hobson's Choice* should contrast with her sister's more frivolous and fashionable outfits. Costumes can be borrowed, made, or, if the budget will allow it, hired from professional costumiers. Costumes need not always be historically accurate, but research into the period in which the play is set, and pictures of previous productions of the play will demonstrate the range of choices open to the costume designer.

If you have chosen costume design as one of your examination options it will be essential to keep a record of your work. Include:

■ Research into costumes of the period or culture in which the play is set

■ Preliminary sketches

■ Fabric and colour samples

■ Budget and health and safety considerations

■ Several costume designs for the performance

■ A justification for your choice of costume designs.

Both AQA and Edexcel require candidates to prepare or construct at least one costume that has been made or assembled for a devised or scripted performance.

 MAKE UP

Skilful make-up will enhance the effects of the costumes, and will help to create a sense of the age of a character, as well as their position in society. It should seem a natural part of the character, unless the play is non-naturalistic, and you are aiming for a specific effect. For example, the Governor and his Wife in *The Caucasian Chalk Circle* might wear very exaggerated, mask-like make-up. Hobson in *Hobson's Choice* is hot-tempered and fond of drink and this might be suggested by a high facial colour. However, it's important to remember that too much make-up can be worse than too little. The effect of make-up and costumes should always be tested under the stage lights.

A portfolio of your designs for make up might include:

- Research notes
- Photographs and illustrations
- Individual make-up designed for the various characters, including beards and hair-styles
- Budgetary considerations
- Your reasons for choosing to emphasize particular features
- An evaluation of your contribution to the success of the scene.

MASKS

Masks have been used since the earliest days of theatre, although they are less frequently seen on the modern stage. There are many kinds of masks, including full-face masks, eye-masks, and half-face masks, and each type produces a different theatrical effect and fulfils a different purpose. Masks may be used for comic or grotesque effect, or to suggest a limited or stereo-typed character. The smaller the mask, the easier it is to design and make, and the more comfortable it will be to wear. It is important to remember that wearing a mask will affect your acting. A full–face mask may reduce the power of your voice and limit your vision. Half-masks, as worn in the Commedia dell' Arte, are easier to design and use.

Naturalistic plays seldom offer opportunities for the use of masks. It is unlikely, for example, that one could use masks effectively in *A Taste of Honey*. On the other hand, in *The Caucasian Chalk Circle* the Governor and his Wife, and even the soldiers and palace officials might wear full or half masks.

If you choose to work on masks as an examination option you will need to:

- Research the use of masks in other times and cultures
- Try to find examples of plays written especially to be performed in masks
- Choose a play or scene that offers possibilities for the use of masks
- Justify your decision to use masks in this scene or play
- Explain why you have chosen a particular style of mask
- Design and make several masks to be used in performance
- Comment on any problems you encountered in making the masks
- Explain the challenges the masks present to the performers
- Evaluate the success of the masks you created and their effect in the production.

PUPPETS

Puppets offer a tremendous range of possibilities, from finger puppets, through glove puppets, to marionettes and rod puppets, to life-size puppets. Even living actors can represent puppets if they are manipulated by other actors and take no responsibility for the control of their own movements. Many plays have been specially written to be performed by puppets, from *Punch and Judy* to the elaborate Bunraku puppet plays of Japan.

It is possible to adapt scenes written for human actors so that they can be performed effectively by puppets. For example, look at the section on Exploring and Comparing the Four Extracts, Section E. Present the poem *My Rules* as an encounter between two glove puppets. Alternatively, in Devised Performance, Section L, you could use puppets to illustrate your explorations of the theme. For example, you might stage a wedding scene where the Bride and Groom are manipulated like puppets by their respective parents.

Remember that to operate any puppet successfully requires considerable practice.

- Research the use of puppets in other times and cultures
- Choose a play or scene that offers possibilities for performance by puppets
- Justify your decision to use a particular style of puppet
- Design and make several puppets to be used in performance

- Comment on any problems you encountered
- Evaluate the success of the puppets you created and their effect in the production.

PROPS

Props, or 'stage properties', usually refer to the portable objects found on stage – items of food, crockery, weapons, telephones, small pieces of furniture, etc. Some will be actually handled or carried by the actors, like Jo's ring in *A Taste of Honey*, and others will be used to add detail to the set. It is important that you provide the actors with at least temporary props to use during rehearsal. In choosing particular props, it is important to work closely with the director and the person designing the set.

- List any props mentioned in the text in order of their appearance.
- What props do the actors actually need?
- What additional props might help them to communicate their character's intentions to the audience?
- Find or create the props that are essential to the scene.
- Make sure that props are functional and available when needed by the actors.
- Make a prop copy of the play that could be used in a production.

STAGE MANAGEMENT

An efficient stage manager is essential to a successful presentation. The stage manager works alongside the director in all aspects of the rehearsal and production, liaising among all the different aspects of the production. The stage manager is responsible for the organization and smooth operation of everything that happens backstage in a performance and is a vital member of the production team. An effective stage manager will be a good communicator, very well organized and able to work as part of a team, as well as to respond quickly to any changes of plan. If you take on this important task you must be prepared to keep track of all the choices made by the director and performers, and especially any decisions taken with regard to the technical side of the production. You must be prepared to accept and deal with any difficulties that arise, either in rehearsal or in production.

It will be your job to keep a Stage Manager's plot or book, containing diagrams for the stage arrangements for each scene, as well as summaries of other plots, such as lighting or props. You will draw up a rehearsal schedule and make sure that the actors are given up to date information about rehearsals. Most importantly you will need to keep notes about all the artistic and staging decisions taken during rehearsal. If you are working with an Assistant Stage Manager or a team, you must make sure that the jobs you have delegated, for example taking responsibility for props or furniture, are efficiently carried out.

If you decide to undertake Stage Management as an examination option, all your rehearsal and performance notes and your plot can be included in your portfolio. You will also need to:

- Comment on any challenges you encountered in rehearsal or performance
- Mention the ways in which you responded to these challenges
- Evaluate the success of your stage management objectively
- Make clear what you have learned from your efforts
- Explain what you might do differently in the future.

LIGHTING

The purpose of stage lighting is to serve the performance and aid communication between actors and audience. Light is closely related to sound – the actor who is difficult to see will usually be difficult to hear. Basic lighting of the stage area is only the beginning of the many dramatic possibilities that effective lighting can offer. You can achieve direction, focus, and atmosphere by the imaginative use of the available stage lighting resources. For example, light flooding from the trapdoor or the entrance to the workshop will help to focus attention on Will Mossop's entrances and exits in *Hobson's Choice*. A flickering red light on the backdrop will suggest warfare in *The Caucasian Chalk Circle*.

If you have taken responsibility for designing the lighting for a scene, build up a portfolio of all the work relating to your task. Include:

- Research into accessible and appropriate lighting sources
- The range and possibilities of the lanterns, gels, gobbos, etc. that are available
- A lighting plot
- The reasons for all your decisions in terms of using lighting to create atmosphere and special effects.

〔ᶜ♫ SOUND

The use of music and sound effects in theatre enhances the atmosphere and helps to create the 'world of the play', but it must be appropriate to the style of the play and integrated effectively into the production. It is unusual to use music in naturalistic plays, yet Joan Littlewood, for example, used an orchestra on stage during the first production of the naturalistic play *A Taste of Honey*. Sometimes the playwright suggests the use of music to provide emotional emphasis at particular moments in the play. Many plays include songs, for example Brecht's *The Caucasian Chalk Circle*. Incidental music, before the play starts, or during an interval, can do more than just entertain the audience. It can be used to create an emotional atmosphere, alert the audience to the style of the scene and suggest the period in which the play is set.

Particular sound effects may be important in a scene. A recording of shouts and screams, gunfire or other effects will help to heighten the sense of confusion during the opening scene of *The Caucasian Chalk Circle*. More domestic sound effects will help to establish both the setting and period of *Hobson's Choice*. In both cases, these effects must be very carefully timed so as to avoid competing with the actors' voices.

Although it is possible to get professional recordings of sound effects, for examination purposes you may be required to create original sound effects and justify their use within the scene. It will help to develop some knowledge of recording sound as well as such skills as editing, play-back, mixing, amplification and balance. A portfolio should include:

- The sound requirements of the scene
- A cue sheet
- A final sound tape
- An explanation of your choice of music and/or sound effects
- An evaluation of the effectiveness of your contribution to the performance.